HAPPY THE LAND

DATE DUE

SE 27'08			
GAYLORD			PRINTED IN U.S.A.

LOUISE DICKINSON RICH

HAPPY
THE LAND

DOWN EAST BOOKS

CAMDEN, MAINE

Publishers, Inc.

l.

Cheverie

ie Litterer

en, Maine

LIBRARY OF CONGRESS CATALOGING-IN-PUBLICATION DATA

Rich, Louise Dickinson, 1903–
    Happy the land / Louise Dickinson Rich.
        p.   cm.
    Originally published: Philadelphia: Lippincott, 1950.
    ISBN 0-89272-452-8 (pbk.)
    1. Middle Dam Region (Me.)—Social life and customs.
    2. Middle Dam Region (Me.)—biography. 3. Country life—
    Maine—Middle Dam Region. 4. Rich, Louise Dickinson,
    1903– . I. Title.
    F29.M57R52 1998
    974.1'75—dc21   98-8791
                                                        CIP

To My Daughter Dinah

BOOKS BY LOUISE DICKINSON RICH

CONTENTS

Foreword

For the past twelve years, I have lived on the **Rapid River**, a beautiful and torrential stream connecting the last two of the Rangeley lakes, Lower Richardson and Umbagog, in this extreme northwestern portion of **Maine**. All about lie thousands of acres of pathless woodland, dotted with swamps and crossed by brooks and lakes. There are no roads with the exception of a five-mile carry between the lakes, made necessary by the fact that the river is not navigable, even by canoe. I started living here when I met and married Ralph. I was on a canoe trip with some friends at the time I met him, and we passed a camp which had obviously just been opened. There were shutters still on some of the windows and the encroaching trees about the buildings spoke eloquently of a long period of neglect. But smoke was rising from the chimney and a man was splitting wood in the yard; so we stopped to pass the time of day with him.

He had owned the place, Forest Lodge, for a long time, but had been unable to come East from Chicago, where he lived, for many years until that very day. Now he was planning to make it his permanent home, a project which he was well aware would involve hard work and discomfort and possibly at times actual deprivation. He invited us to lunch and I listened to him talk about the life on which he was embarking. It sounded good to me, and so did he. Eight months after that we were married.

Forest Lodge is truly isolated. The nearest neighbors are at Middle Dam, two miles up the rough and narrow Carry Road, leading from the so-called hotel—it is really a fairly elaborate fishing camp—to Sunday Cove on Umbagog. There isn't anything at all at Sunday Cove except a shack with a woods telephone in it. At Middle Dam there are two families, the Parsons who run the hotel and the Millers who tend the dam, with whatever hired help they may currently be employing. The population hovers between nine and twelve souls, except in summer when the hotel is open and the place is flooded with what we call "sports." In summer we can ride to Middle in one of the jallopies that Ralph, through some impressive miracles of mechanical savvy, kept running; but in winter we have to snowshoe, carrying on our backs the mail and the groceries. At any time of year there is no connection with the Outside—or civilization—except by boat and car, or snow boat and car, depending on the reason. Andover boasts the nearest Post Office, eighteen miles away, and the nearest shopping center of any pretension at all is Rumford, forty difficult miles from home. We don't gad about the stores very much.

We three families can talk with each other over a lumber-company's private woods line, a battery-operated affair whose single strand of uninsulated wire dips and sags into brook and snowdrift and is constantly menaced by falling trees across its fifteen-mile length. And we can talk with Joe Mooney over at the Brown Farm, the company's local head-quarters and clearinghouse for news, ailing horses, and disgruntled woodsmen. Joe sits in the middle of a network of wires and talks with remote lumber camps and wardens' shacks and damkeepers' houses, and keeps his finger on the pulse of the woods. If you want to know where a forest fire is, or when the game warden is apt to be In, you just call up Joe.

During the first three years we lived at Forest Lodge we were alone, except for Gerrish, whom I suppose I will have to call the hired man. Actually he was much more than that. He was a friend and a member of the family. That's the only kind of help you can have in this country, so remote from movies and stores and other forms of amusement. There's nothing for a man to do in his off-time if he is to be excluded from the family circle. So you have to have a practical rule that anyone who isn't good enough to sit in your living-room, evenings, and read and talk and listen to the radio with you, isn't good enough to work for you at all. It pans out very well.

At the end of three years, on a December night that I won't soon forget, our son Rufus was born. His father was in sole attendance on the occasion, since Gerrish had gone Out on vacation, and there was no time to be fooling around getting doctors. After the initial jitters and the ensuing half-hour in which he was hopping around like a cat on a griddle, heating water that he never used and greasing the baby with machine oil, Ralph felt very much pleased with his prowess as a midwife. You'd have thought that Rufus was the first baby ever born. He came equipped with a caul, and this feature was, of course, the result of Ralph's cleverness and to his personal credit. Five years after that our daughter Dinah was born, but I went to a hospital for that affair. No use crowding your luck too far,

I decided. And when Dinah was a few months old, we added Catherine and her little boy Vaughn to the menage. Catherine is Gerrish's married daughter, and when her husband was called into the service, she came to work for me for the duration. In addition, we had Kyak, the one dog left of a team of huskies that sounded like a good idea but wasn't, and a cat named Tom. So we lived for three years.

Then the bottom dropped out of my life. Ralph died, not after an illness during which I would have had time to prepare heart and mind for the bleak time to come, but suddenly, between one breath and the next, on a still and snowy December night. We were alone together at Forest Lodge, since Catherine and the children were staying in a house we'd rented in Andover so Rufus and Vaughn could attend school. I think I need not tell what a terrible and shocking thing it was for me, nor underline the sense of hopelessness and loss that pervaded my days for months after that. Many adults have suffered a like loss at some time during their lives, and they will understand without words from me. I can only say that in time I began to live again, and that it was truly a rebirth; for all the things I'd loved about this life here, all the places Ralph and I had been together and the things we had done were restored with a freshness that was not the freshness of novelty, but better than that—the clear definition of new vision brought to bear on things old and precious through association and memory and experience.

So I decided that I would write a book to please myself, about the things I love, while they still shone so brightly.

This is that book.

HAPPY THE LAND

CHAPTER I

Happy the Land

I WAS BROUGHT up in eastern Massachusetts where every stone is stained with the blood of a patriot, every ancient elm once shaded a treaty signing, every highway once rang to the pounding urgency of a Revere. The sod of the wide lawns surrounding the beautiful Colonial houses is steeped in tradition, and the very air one breathes is mellow with the past. The weight of history lies upon everything.

Therefore this country was strange to me when I came here to live twelve years ago. It was wild and new. It had no past, in the accepted sense of the word. The lakes lay innocent of historical significance and the forested mountains bore no scars of empire-altering events. It was a place, it seemed to me, almost without meaning in the march of human destiny; there were no landmarks; there was nothing to which to tie. The only stories told of the land were— no matter how far back they dated—purely personal stories, like the tale of Metalluk, for whom a brook and an island are named.

Metalluk was an Indian and he lived with his wife Oozalluk on Pine Island up in the Narrows. When Oozalluk died in the middle of winter, Metalluk could not, of course, bury her, since the ground was frozen solid and covered with snow besides. So he wrapped her up in birch bark and suspended her over the smoke vent of his cabin, a procedure not so outlandish as it sounds. That was the usual Indian method of embalming a hundred years ago. When spring came, he ran her body down to Lake Umbagog in his canoe, and buried it on what is now called Metalluk Island.

After that he lived around here for years, and there are many stories told about him. I guess the one that impresses me most is the report of how he stopped at various farms at various times to beg one bullet, because he wanted to shoot a deer. If anyone offered him more than one bullet he was insulted. He'd draw himself up and announce that he was no game hog. He only wanted one deer. To one like me, whose marksmanship is of the variety that necessitates the filling of the air about the target with tons of flying lead on the off-chance that one slug may conceivably strike home, this attitude smacks of lunacy.

Metalluk suddenly went blind and was found in his remote cabin up near Parmachene by two trappers. He was near the point of death, being unable to hunt or to help himself in any way. He'd had a tame moose penned up near the hut, but he'd managed to tear down one side of the pen and free the animal, early in his blindness, because he could no longer feed and water it, and he couldn't bear to have it starve. This doesn't sound like the Indians of the literature of my youth—those cruel and bloodthirsty red varmints—but that's what he did, all the same.

The trappers took him home to Stewartstown and he was auctioned off as a town pauper, a method of caring for public charges in those days. At the Town Meeting the town poor were bid off for the ensuing year, the lowest bidder becoming responsible for the board and lodging of the individual, and being bound to return him to the town at the end of the period as well clothed as when he had been taken. Metalluk was bid off annually for several years, for sums ranging from $29 (to a Leonard Fellows) to $48.25 (to a Howard Blodgett). He finally died and is buried in Stewartstown.

Now this is to me a very sad story about a very interesting and remarkable character; but it's a story of no historical import, except insofar as the tracing of the decline of a proud man from a life of freedom and physical independence to the lot of a helpless town pauper, and how he managed under those circumstances to retain his dignity and his spiritual independence—and Metalluk did—may have implications. No battles were lost or won because of Metalluk, nor were any Acts of Congress passed. Nobody ever heard of him, except around here.

That is true of all the stories that can be told about this country. They are all purely personal history. That's the only kind of history a country like this, so far off the beaten track, so lacking in any commodity worth fighting for—according to political or trade standards—can possibly have. Each of us here must write his own history of the territory, establish his own landmarks, honor his own anniversaries, create his own traditions. And that is what we have done, unintentionally and by degrees, during the past twelve years. Of Plymouth Rock, I may tell my children: "This is where the Pilgrims landed." Of the rock by the side of the road, halfway up Wangan Hill, I say, "Right here is where your father found the little deer that time."

I made a map once of the five-mile length of the Carry Road, from the front yard of the hotel, down past the Chub Pool trail, through Black Valley and up Birch Hill, past the Wangan and Forest Lodge, past Smooth Lodge and Spike, down at last to Sunday Cove, where there is a ledge, a Brown Company shack with a telephone in it, a pair of loons, and a sad-looking boathouse in which we used to store the Chris-craft. It was my intention at the time to mark with an X and the date each spot on the road where we had come to grief in one of the many senile objects we optimistically call cars. At that time we had a Model T, an ailing 1917 Packard, and a temperamental 1924 Marmon, known locally as the "Mormon." After that we got an old Essex, a very old Model A, and a very, very old Reo, and I gave up my map making for plain lack of space in which to make any more X's. It didn't make any difference anyhow. I can remember in painful detail every catastrophe that overtook us along that five miles of ruts and encroaching brush and collapsed corduroy culverts.

I can remember, for example, standing at the foot of Wangan Hill with tears of pure agony running down my face and freezing as they ran, while I tried to warm my aching hands by thrusting them under my sheepskin. I had to get them warm and go back to my job as mechanic's helper. We *had* to get to Middle Dam before the semi-monthly mail went out—this was before the palmy days of the Star Route—and the bands on that fool Model T had gone. If you've never changed Model T bands in sub-zero weather, don't. It's a fate worse than death. Of all the ungodly mechanical makeshifts, that Model T band racket was the worst. But I shouldn't speak ill of the dead, I suppose.

I can remember standing in a haze of heat and black flies, trying to get the pump out of the Packard. It had to be possible. The builders had got it in somehow, hadn't they? But the space allotted just wasn't wide enough. Ralph had said to me, "Here, see if you can get this Christly thing out. I've fooled with it for an hour. We've *got* to get it out."

"What makes you think I can do it?" I asked. "I'm not the mechanic."

"No, but you've got more patience than I have." That's a line husbands pull. If it's the landlord to be jacked up about the broken cellar step, *you* take it up with him, because you have more tact. If it's the bore next door come in to chat, *you* talk to him, because you can always think of something to say. If it's the son and heir to be disciplined, *you* do it, because you can be uglier than I can. We all know that line.

As usual, easily flattered fool that I am, I fell for it. At the end of another hour I hadn't a fingernail to my name, my arms were gudgeon grease to the elbow, my eyes were swollen to slits by fly bites, and my famous patience lay in flinders about my feet. At that inauspicious moment Ralph strolled up behind me, looking cool and calm—flies didn't bite him; he'd developed an immunity over the years—and asked in a voice of detached interest, "Well, how're you doing?"

I looked over my shoulder. "May the pits of the nether hell—" I began, and stopped. Something had happened. I looked back at my hands. They were outside the chassis and the pump was in them, free and clear. Don't ask me how it got there. I don't know. I couldn't do it again. But I never go past a certain spruce near a rock on the left-hand side of the Carry Road below Long Pool without remembering that right there I had a telling demonstration of the deliberate orneriness of the inanimate.

I never go by a special, rotting old pumpkin-pine stump with an eighteen inch fir courageously starting a life of its own atop it, without remembering that right there the trailer, full of our entire winter's supply of canned goods, broke loose from the hitch, flew off at a tangent through the woods, came up whamo against a boulder, and exploded in forty directions. That was a mess.

I never cross Black Valley Brook, where the road for some reason cants gently off to the north, without recalling the grief following the day the Packard fell off the carry. We thought we'd never get it out of the brook, but by the grace of God and a long-handled spoon, plus a few cant dogs and a team of horses, we did.

The pitch up from Long Pool means to me that we are almost home from Sunday Cove, and that that's where the Marmon dropped her transmission, an accident which proved fatal. She never went on the road again, thank God, but has spent the rest of her days powering the carriage of the sawmill. I never liked that Marmon, anyway, but Ralph went into full mourning for a week. I always thought, although I have no way of proving it—and far be it from me to pry into the past of any husband of mine—that the chief reason for his sorrow was that the car had a great sentimental value to him, from the good old days when he was free, white, and twenty-one. It must have been a swell parking car. I wouldn't know about that myself. I was only the wife, and what time I spent in the back seat was devoted to watching out the rear window to see if the trailer was following as it should and to sound the tocsin if the chair we'd lashed onto the peak of an already too large load started to slip its moorings.

The assorted griefs of the Carry Road were not confined to the road itself. Its baleful influence was potent enough to extend beyond its terminals. It was off the Middle Dam dock that Raymond Parsons, Howard Dunning, and Jum Hutchins spent an hour of jeopardy. They had started from South Arm during the spring breakup with the idea of getting into Middle Dam and going to work for Captain Coburn, who then ran the hotel. At that time of the year the ice is not safe, so they had the sound-seeming notion of hauling a canoe full of duffle behind them on a hand sled for the four miles. Then if the ice gave out, they could jump into the canoe. This was one of those ideas that appears good and reasonable, but is not, in practice, completely satisfactory.

We were all at Middle when they showed up down the lake, tugging and hauling through the slush. It looked like hard work. Just off the dock they gave the assembled multitude of seven souls a triumphant hail. At that point the ice began to give, rotted as it was by the sun and fretted by the current, and, faithful to their plan, they all jumped into the canoe. They were safe and dry, but they hadn't taken into consideration the fact that you can't break eight inches of even rotten ice with a canoe. They were stuck. They couldn't paddle and they couldn't walk. There they sat, thrashing desperately with their paddles and hitching in concert and getting no place fast, while we all shouted worthless advice. It didn't help matters at all when everyone finally collapsed with laughter. In the end, Raymond got out and pushed, bearing most of his weight on the gunwale, and so at last they came ashore. Now if we have to cross the lakes during the breakup, we go around. It's longer and harder, but you're surer of getting there.

The other end of the carry, at Sunday Cove, was the scene of one of my own less happy hours, and it involved the Chris-craft. Possibly the fact that, the minute I got into the thing, I always started expecting the worst to happen was responsible for the worst always happening. There can be something in atmosphere, I suppose. On this occasion Ralph and I had gone to Errol Dam to see Cleve West about taking up the clutch, which was slipping, and fixing the lights, which never had worked since we owned the boat. This shouldn't have taken very long, only Ralph and Cleve are both nuts about mechanics, and they never could get together and consummate a plain business deal in a reasonable length of time. They always had to get technical about the flaws in the construction of the town's new tractor, or the need in this world for a different and better tire iron. So we never did leave there until hours after we should have.

Then we had to go to Middle Dam to get the groceries. At the time our household, at Pine Point, numbered twenty-three, and twenty-three people, some of whom are workmen and some of whom are growing children, manage to get outside quite a lot of food in a day's time. The larder was wearing thin in spots. The groceries had to be brought down. When we got back to the Cove, the Ford wouldn't start, so we had to fix that. By the time we got to Middle, it was six o'clock; so I called Catherine up and told her to serve supper. We'd eat at the hotel and come right down afterward. So far, so good. We ate, loaded the goods, and set off again for the Cove. It began to get dark and we discovered that the Ford's lights wouldn't work. However, by not sparing the horses, we did get back to the Chris-craft just as the last light was draining out of the sky. It was already dark in the woods, but on Umbagog it was still light enough so that we thought we could probably get home without running ashore. We loaded crate after crate of food into the back cockpit until it was level full, climbed aboard, and shoved off. Ralph stepped on the starter, threw her into reverse—and nothing happened except a simply frightful clatter. He cut the power and sat looking baffled and defeated.

Then I heard water gurgling. I went haywire. "Lemme out of here!" I shrieked and made a flying leap over intervening space onto the ledge. I may sound like the fussy type, but I don't like to have boats sink under me or to be thrown into the water unprepared. I'm not afraid of water and I can swim adequately if not stylishly. Rufus once told a neighbor who was admonishing him for jumping into the river fully clad, "My mother won't care. She goes in the water all the time with her clothes on." It was perfectly true; only I like to do it on purpose and not by accident.

"For God's sake," Ralph howled, "don't let her get away." He threw me the painter and I towed her in and tied her up. The water continued to gurgle in increasing volume, and we located the leak by sound as being under the floor boards of the back cockpit. We looked at each other sickly. We'd have to unload all those tons of freight, and we'd have to do it fast. Not only was the boat about to sink, but the light was almost gone. We started heaving cases and crates over the side in a gloom which on closer inspection proved to be the beginning of a thunderstorm and not just plain nightfall.

Finally we discovered the trouble. When Ralph had shifted, the pin had come out of the shaft which had worked back—I *hope* I've got this right—leaving a hole through which the water was pouring and dropping the propeller into the rudder. If we'd made up our minds we could keep afloat, we still couldn't have gone anywhere, having neither propelling agency nor steering ability. All this was brought to light by the aid of matches. Ralph said, "This is a hell of a note. Look, get out on the back deck and see if you can shove the shaft in while I try to put the pin back."

I lay prone on the deck, plunged my arm in the water up to the shoulder, and found that the tips of my fingers would just touch one blade of the propeller. I couldn't get any purchase and I couldn't exert any pressure. I know of no more irritating a situation. If you could only get your feet on something solid, you have the feeling then you could do business. I started undressing. "I've got to go overboard," I told Ralph. "Hold it a minute."

He made a token protest. "You don't want to do that."

"Certainly I don't want to do it," I assured him crossly, "but I guess I've got to." I slid over the side into eight feet of water, which was not too awfully cold after all. I could feel what I was trying to do pretty well, in spite of the, now, pitch blackness. I couldn't get my feet on the bottom, but even so, I was doing all right when something began nibbling gently at me. "Something's biting me," I said nervously. "Are pickerel carnivorous?"

Ralph's voice came hollowly from the space under the deck. "Oh, probably it's only bloodsuckers."

They heard me shriek in Berlin (N. H.) and I came out of the lake so fast the water boiled. "Don't be a damn fool," Ralph requested shortly. "They won't hurt you. Give her another shove and a quarter turn to the left." Shuddering, I reinserted myself into Umbagog and tried to shove and do a bloodsucker-discouraging shimmy at the same time. I could hear Ralph swearing under his breath between orders to turn left or right; and just when I'd decided I couldn't stand my situation a minute longer, he grunted "O.K." I got

out of there fast, threw my clothes back on, and started re-
loading groceries. "You'd better call home," Ralph said,
"and tell them to leave a lantern on the float. We'll never
find it otherwise." So I used the phone in the Brown Company shack, got aboard, and we started.

You couldn't see your hand in front of your face, except
when the lightning flashed, and then the ensuing darkness
was worse than ever; but we got out of the Cove all right,
more by good luck than good navigation. Ralph speeded
her up a little. "Hey!" I exclaimed apprehensively. "You're
too far to the left." Remarks like "port your helm," or
whatever it is, leave me flat in a crisis with only my land-
lubberly vocabulary, which, however, does serve.

"Oh, no, we're——" he began, and the bow of the boat
crashed into something that raked the keel with a sickening
sound. The propeller grated and thrashed crazily, and we
lost all momentum. Ralph cut the motor. I gave up. Obviously this was my night to die in the wet dark. We both sat
there, wordless. There was nothing to say. I listened for the
sound of flooding water, but heard nothing. After a long
minute we began to breathe again and Ralph stepped on
the starter. She turned over slowly and we found, with
complete surprise, that we still had steerageway, if you can
call the pace of a grandmother snail steerageway.

"Now what?" Ralph asked in a conversational tone. "We
don't really want to run onto any more reefs, do we?"

I thought we didn't.

"Take her over toward the New Hampshire side," I suggested. "Maybe we can see the lantern on the float from
there."

"Maybe we can if we can find New Hampshire."

We limped in the direction we thought, maybe, was west

and saw dimly in the distance a faint flicker of light, to the south. "That's it," Ralph stated. "Now if we can manage to keep off that Brandy Point reef——"

With that the thunderstorm broke. The heavens opened and the rain came down in sheets. The lantern disappeared—whether screened by rain or extinguished we could not know. "Well," said Ralph mildly, "if we don't drown one way we can another. I'm breathing water right now."

Then we saw a flashlight off our port bow. No one will ever know how good it looked to us. "You all right?" came Fred Tibbott's voice. "Dave and I thought we'd better come look for you." Dave is his brother and they were visiting us at the time. "We'll pilot you in if you'll cut down to canoe speed." We laughed hoarsely. Cut down to canoe speed indeed!

So we finally got home, and our homecoming was the only nice thing about that trip. The rain had stopped and the entire household was lined up on the edge of the float with every lantern and light in the place. It looked like a carnival. All the girls—there were eight there then—were wearing what amounted to their uniform, shorts and shirts, and I'll never forget how pretty that row of slim brown legs looked in the watery lantern light. It's a silly thing to remember, but I do.

There are so many things to remember about my country—so many things that aren't important to anyone else. What is important about standing in the snow, feeling terribly happy as I once did? I don't even know why I felt so good on that occasion. I'd walked to Middle to get the mail after lunch on a beautiful, high, blue and white day. I'd sat around and chopped it up with Alys Parsons for a while, and just as I was ready to go home, Larry came in with a load of wood. "Wait till I unload," he said, "and I'll give you a lift down as far as my woodlot." So I waited.

We stood on the rack behind the slowly pacing horses and exchanged commonplaces. It was when we parted at the point where his road leaves the carry that I remember. I climbed down, kicked my snowshoes on, wiggled into the straps of the pack-basket, and whistled Kyak away from the horses. Then I looked up to say good-bye, and suddenly I felt good. The horses stood there rippling their great dappled rumps in the light stir of air. They were steaming gently and tossing their heads so that the harness creaked and jangled a little. Larry loafed on the sled with the easy, wide-footed grace of a teamster, his wool mittens bright against the leather of his apron, his eyes laughing and narrowed against the sun, his head outlined sharply against the shouting blue of the winter sky. The lavender shadows of the bare trees lay in a pattern across the faintly golden snow, across the horses and the sled, across Kyak prancing impatiently around. I even remember what we were saying. I said, "If you find you can't haul the stuff down Saturday, call us up"; and he said, "I'll do that, Louise." And all the time I was feeling wonderful—and at last it occurs to me why—to be living in a country where men at routine work unconsciously and unknowingly fall into living masterpieces of line and color and significance as classic and as lovely as painted masterpieces like, for example, "The Gleaners."

Every time I look across the river in winter to the little island on the other side, I remember a lot of things that happened there. I remember a silly sport Ralph and I indulged in, all of one winter—the last full winter we had there before he died. That was a terrible winter for snow.

The Sunday before Thanksgiving it started to fall, and snowed an inch an hour for forty hours, conclusively bottling us up for the winter. Of course we had the usual regulation snow on top of that. That was only a super-de-luxe special for this November only. But we had snowshoes and we could get about. The deer could not and the poor things were yarding up and starving to death. One of the yards was on the island, in plain view of our kitchen windows. A deeryard, by the way, is not an open space like a corral, but a thick interlacing of beaten down runways in which the deer mill about, and a series of hollows under bushes in which they sleep. We watched them every day for a while, saw them getting thinner and thinner as they browsed off all the branches within their highest reach; and finally, out of pure inability to take the sight of animals dying before our eyes, we struggled over there one day and cut down a lot of cedars so they'd have something to eat. Eating cedar makes a deer taste like furniture polish if you come to butcher him, but we had no such notions, so it didn't matter. After that we felt they owed us something in the way of entertainment, so we started whistling and waving to them whenever we were bored. Deer are very dull animals, in spite of their grace and beauty, and they'd just stand there and stare at us blankly, looking simple. We finally discovered that we could hypnotize them by this waving and whistling gag, and then we'd sneak off and leave them staring across the churning rapids at nothing.

"Gosh, we're mean," said Ralph. "But I'll bet you that big buck will be here if we come back in ten minutes." So every day we'd make a book on the length of time a chosen favorite would stand. A big doe of my fancy established a record of twenty-three minutes.

"Judas," I said, "isn't she stupid! Imagine a person looking at space for twenty-three minutes."

Ralph cocked a sardonic eye. "You haven't been around much, Babe, have you? I can name, without trying, at least four——"

"Aw right, aw right," I said. Come to think of it, so could I. Come to think twice, I wasn't too awfully sure I didn't head his list.

I almost spent the rest of my life on the island once. The only way to get onto it is to cross the dam up above, follow the shore line down about a quarter of a mile, and jump the back channel at the one point where it is narrow enough. Usually this is simple—just one wholehearted leap from one flat rock, over four feet of boiling current, onto another flat rock. If you miss, you get wet, but what of it? One spring, however, before the ice was out, we decided to go over to the island and see if the eight-by-eight timbers that had washed up during the winter—the river never freezes; it's too swift—were as sound and good as they looked to be from our side. If they were, we wanted them. There was a lot of water running, due to the spring rains and the melting snow, and the leap onto the island was a lot longer than it had been. But it was not impossible, even to me. We investigated the timbers, decided they weren't worth the bother, and took a look at the old corduroy road that had always so intrigued us.

It led from one side of the island, the thirty or forty feet, to the other. Why? It was old, old, old. The only reason it hadn't long since rotted away was that it was made of cedar. Who built it? Where did they think they were going? The woods on either side of the river were virgin, with no trace of a road anywhere. We had tried to pin it on Benedict

Arnold, but everyone said we were crazy. He never came anywhere near here. An old man I met once told me that in his father's youth there had been a road from Canada to Bethel, and his father could remember when he was young seeing trains of fifty and a hundred people trooping over it to the Bethel Fair. They had prize cattle and drove flocks of geese and camped every night by the roadside and held dances to the music of fiddles. Maybe, he said, this was a piece of that road. But no one else ever heard of such a thing, so perhaps he made it up. I hope, though, that it was true. It sounds wonderful.

Be that as it may, we looked at the road, speculated a bit more about it, and started home. It was then that I discovered what had not before been apparent in all the years I had been making that jump. The shore-side rock was about six inches higher than the island rock. I'd jumped down onto the island and up onto the mainland a hundred times and not known it. It hadn't made any difference, with only four feet to go. Now it made all the difference. I looked at the six feet of snarling water between me and safety and I knew I couldn't do it. Below lay a nasty deep pool full of grinding ice. If I ever fell into that—and I would, sure as God made little apples—I would sink like a frozen stone.

"I can't make it," I said to Ralph, who had negotiated the breach with no trouble at all. He was six foot three, with long legs.

"Don't be silly. Of course you can. Come on, Babe. Quit fooling around and jump."

I looked again, drew myself together, got ready to jump, and felt my knees turn to jelly. Did you ever try to dive from a high board? Did you ever find that the longer you stood there, screwing up your courage, the more impossible the dive became? That was me. "I *can't,*" I quavered—I, who never quaver.

"Damn it, of course you can. Do you want to stay there until the Fourth of July?"

I didn't, but—— "Do something!" I begged.

He turned on his heel. "I'll go home and get you a sandwich and a blanket, if you're determined to lay out there for the next two months." And the stinker stalked off and left me.

That had the desired effect. "Wait for Mama!" I shrieked, closed my eyes, and took off. I landed with four inches to spare; but since then I've been pretty particular about the conditions under which I go onto the island.

Just to keep the record straight about that piece of corduroy—myself, I like all ends tied up, if possible—it's gone now. It went out the next spring when Pondy Dam washed away. That was the day! My attitude toward catastrophes is that I don't really hope they'll happen, but if they have to, I hope I'll be there to see. I was there to see the dam go. We all stood on the bank and watched, and suddenly the fill and the toe piling dissolved. Water poured through the breach with the roaring abandon of a runaway express train, and the walkways of the dam screeched, bent, and splintered. The noise and speed of the unleashed river were terrifying, and at the same time intoxicating. I'm a fool for rushing water—I could watch it for hours in a state of hypnotism—but this was a little too much. A whole family of mink that had been living in one of the piers and stealing the fish that successful anglers trustingly laid down on the walkway jumped into the flood and battled their way ashore. All the river drivers ran along the bank and tried to save them. Mink are vicious, but these were too hard pressed to have time or energy to bite. A bird that had its nest in the eaves of the dam sat there and sang like an idiot while its world washed out from under it. We thought it was going to drown, but it didn't. At the last minute it gave a bewildered squawk and rose into the air. It circled over the churning water for a long time, and then it flew away.

After a while Ralph and I remembered that we had a water pump down on the riverbank, which by now had probably been washed away, too. So we went home. The pump was all right. It was under three feet of water, but we managed to get it out before any really sizable flotsam rammed into it. It was full of silt and gravel, but it could be cleaned, we decided. We looked over at the island just in time to see the corduroy road lift, turn, and go off downriver, breaking up against trees and rocks as it went. It was too bad. It had been there for a long time, longer than anybody or anything in the whole country.

There's a little plot of grass across the road from the Winter House, and I remember sitting there all one afternoon in the interests of what I thought at the time was a Christian deed. Rush Rogers and Phil Haley, two friends of ours who were working on the drive, came down and said, "Say, Louise, if you're not busy, how about taking your book and sitting up by the road? A guy is coming past and he doesn't know his way. Would you hail him and direct him?" I should have known that they were up to no good, but I didn't know them, then, as well as I came to later. So I said I would and took the dogs along for company. They seemed a little restless, darting off into the woods on unexplained errands which involved much barking, but I put that down to spring. Nobody came by at all, and come suppertime,

I called it a day and knocked off. I didn't find out until later about the dirty trick I'd been party to.

It seems there was a party of river drivers rearing—cleaning the grounded logs off the bank—on the other side of the river. They got down as far as Smooth Ledge by quitting time. The walking on the other side is terrible. There was a trail there once, but now it is full of down tops and mud-holes. When the end of the stint came, two of the drivers decided to swim the river at the Ledge and come up the carry, instead of struggling back the hard way. They took off their clothes, wrapped them around stones, and heaved them over. One man's wardrobe landed safely, but the stone fell out of the other's, his clothes all fell into the middle of the river and were whisked away toward Umbagog, leaving him there as naked as a jaybird. He decided very sensibly to swim across, anyhow. Having no clothes gave him all the more reason for not wanting to scramble through thicket and over rock. It wasn't until he smelled the smoke from our chimney that he remembered about me —or as he doubtless put it, although everybody was too polite to tell me so, "that damn woman." River drivers are, as a class, about the most modest people I've ever heard of, and the idea of stalking past in his birthday suit was only slightly more abhorrent than the idea of hailing me from behind a bush and asking me to turn my back for a minute. So he sent his companion along to camp to get him some raiment, and he sat down to wait. He must have been frightfully uncomfortable. It was the middle of black fly season, and that's no joke, even with clothes on.

Now river drivers usually own the clothes they stand in and an extra pair of socks. Our friend was no exception. His pal had to start begging and borrowing a shirt here, a pair of pants there, and some shoes somewhere else. In the course of this project he ran afoul of Rush and Phil. They lured him into the dingle—the shack in which the cook keeps his extra supplies—tied him up, and locked him in. Then they came down and gave me that cock-and-bull story about the stranger who was on his way In.

You see what happened. I sat there for hours effectively keeping that poor, poor man from going home. He tried to circle around me through the woods, but the dogs headed him off every time. Finally he went back to the Ledge, re-swam the river, picked up a rotten grain sack in an old lumber camp to give him assurance, I suppose, and returned to camp the hard way. When he got there, full of wrath and woe, did he get any sympathy? Of course not. Everyone thought it was very funny, except the boss, who gave him hell. It doesn't do a boss's reputation any good to have men drown on his drive, and swimming the river in early June is strictly taboo.

Oh, my own country, my country that I love! I never follow the spring-line back onto the ridge without remembering that right here, where it dips into a mossy little bog, we made "Elizabeth" into a term of censure. I dropped a wrench into a mudhole, and Ralph said severely, "Well, Louise *Elizabeth* Rich! Can't you be trusted with a simple tool?" I said, having no other defense, "My name isn't Elizabeth." He said he knew it wasn't, but when you wanted to reprimand anybody you had to call them by a nice rolling name, and that was Elizabeth. Since then, whenever any of our household is displeased with another member, that's the way—one of the ways—we show it. Sometimes strangers have wondered. It does sound, I suppose, a bit odd to have a wife address her husband coldly as "Ralph Elizabeth."

I never go down the lake in Larry's boat without making a mental note that right here Howard Dunning picked up the little fawn. He saw it through field glasses, saw it swimming in the white-capped blue, saw it weakening and drowning. He put out in a kicker-boat, dragged it aboard, and brought it in. Why it had started to swim the lake we don't really know, but probably wildcats were on its trail. There are a lot of wildcats on the mountain on the other side. It was only a suckling, with the spots still bright and clear as gold coins on its little back. He called me up one afternoon. "Louise, you know that fawn. I can't make it eat. What should I do?"

I didn't really know. I'd never raised a fawn, only a skunk, six puppies, and two children—one, Dinah, still in the suckling bracket herself. But I have my theories about the feeding of young animals. You treat them exactly as you would a baby—and how you find out about that is to read books for inexperienced mothers. "I'll send you up a nursing bottle full of Dinah's formula," I told him. "It may not work, but it can't hurt him. Just canned milk, corn syrup, and water. It won't hurt to try."

It didn't hurt a bit. The fawn loved the formula and the bottle. It grew up and was turned loose, finally. I know where Howard picked it up, but what I really think of when I pass that spot is that the first sharing of Dinah's life was with a bit of animation that had no claims of its own. Nature is ruthless; the fawn should have died. But human nature isn't like that. We care. I like to remember that before she was old enough to know what she was doing, Dinah subscribed to the doctrine that the strong have a responsibility toward the weak.

I am not a complete admirer of the writings of Thomas

Wolfe; I consider him a bit wordy. But out of that very wordiness come sometimes beautiful and provocative phrases that might have been lost through a more extensive editing. One such I remember, although I have long since forgotten the context: "A stone, a leaf, an unfound door; the lost lane-end into heaven." What that meant to Thomas Wolfe I do not know. It has come to have a very personal meaning to me. There is not a leaf or a stone or a bend of road or a sun-glinting stretch of lake or river anywhere here that is not to me a lost lane-end into heaven.

Happy the land, someone has said, that has no history. This is such a land, I suppose. The only history we have is our purely personal history, and I am not sure but what that is the best kind of history there is. In a world which has lately been wiped out in every spiritual and conceptual sense, where whole cities can be destroyed in a moment and whole races subjected to unthinkable things in the name of History, what is there left to be sure of, except your own life, your own memories, your own certitude of decency and hope and happiness on the earth, engendered and fostered by your own experiences? A land without history, I have come to believe, is not a land without meaning.

CHAPTER II

Gerrish

He was a person you'd never know was in the house. For weeks after the day he came to work for us, saying in his diffident way, "My name is Gerrish. Fred Tibbott said maybe you could use a man about the place," I would forget to set a plate for him at the table. He was as easy to forget as the air, as bread, as a rain that falls in the night. He was a little brown man, looking as most countrymen do, ageless —the same at sixty as he had at thirty, old then, young for his age now. He trod lightly and spoke softly. When I wanted him to split wood or carry water, he was there, as silent as a shadow and as faithful. When the need of him was past, he was gone back to his wall building or boat caulking or gardening. He was the hired help and he knew his proper place.

And I knew mine. I was the boss's wife, and I felt then as I still feel, that the paying of money to a man for performing prescribed duties does not carry with it a license to pry into his mind or heart or past. He had enough to attend to anyhow, without sitting around doing what he termed "jawrin' " with me. At half-past five he arose and kindled the kitchen fire, and as soon as the teakettle was on the boil, thumped on the living-room ceiling with the broom handle, making in the room above a bloodcurdling racket which was designed, successfully, to bring me up standing. By the time I'd dressed and arrived in the kitchen, he was in the woodshed splitting wood, and I would see neither hide nor hair of him until I beat on the old circular saw blade which Ralph and I once salvaged from the ruins of a burned-down birch mill and hung by the back door to serve as a dinner gong.

Breakfast at our house consists of everyone's eating and carefully excluding me from any conversation, because, as Gerrish put it, "Louise ain't rightly herself till she's had time to get her feet braced for the day." So I sat and thought my own gloomy thoughts while Ralph and Gerrish discussed the immediate program. There might be the garden to plant or a porch floor to paint or a new roof to be put on the guide's house. Or perhaps the day's activities would extend farther afield—up to Middle Dam to heat-treat a piece of steel in the damkeeper's little smithy, or over the ridge to an abandoned lumber camp, to look for discarded lengths of strap iron, necessary for the completion of some project. If it were the fall of the year, Gerrish might be detailed to spend the day tramping the swamps and upland stands of timber hunting for the deer which every family hereabouts hangs to freeze in an outbuilding against the time when transportation fails and food is impossible to get in from the Outside.

There was a sameness about these breakfast-table convocations. No matter what was asked of him, Gerrish would say, "Cal'late I can manage," or "Hain't never turned my hand to that, but likely I'll make out." That is, unless the driving of one of the junk heaps that we wishfully call cars was involved. He had a tendency, in a crisis, to haul on the reins and shout "Whoa!"—a hang-over from his horse-and-buggy youth. This simply does not work, and he was the first to admit it, saying, "I just don't sympathize with no goddam motor. They don't cotton to me nor me to them." The one exception to this rule was a 3½ h.p. outboard we own, which no one else, not even Ralph who was a mechanical genius, could make run. It ran like a dream for Gerrish. When pressed for the secret of his success he said simply, "Wal, I'm *int'rested* in that motor." Men have a tendency to personify machinery, I have found.

As soon as he'd drained his coffee cup and taken a final doughnut to ballast the lone piece of last night's blueberry pie—which he'd voluntarily eaten to save—he'd be gone. I wouldn't see him again, except for the brief dinner period when conversation dealt exclusively with the excursions and alarums of the morning, until our early supper. Then he'd eat quickly and excuse himself, saying, "Got an idee the salmon might be rising at Long Pool tonight, and I'd like to get in my licks before bedtime." Since his bedtime was self-admittedly: "soon's it's dark under the table," I had very little opportunity, my principles quite aside, of ever becoming acquainted with the man.

So I never even knew he'd had a family until the morning when I was trying to do the washing and make strawberry jam and plan a short story simultaneously. I might possibly have succeeded if it hadn't been for Rufus, then five, who chose that day to be stricken with the complaint common to most lone and lonely children, the "What'll-I-do-now-Mom Blues." He was driving me mad when Gerrish came into the kitchen, gave the situation one experienced glance, and said apologetically, "The Boss claims he wants me to peel them cedar poles. I kind of miss a young one under foot, now my own four are growed, so I was think-in'——"

The cedar poles were in a clearing back of the clothes-yard, so I decided I could more or less check on Gerrish's trustworthiness during my various harried excursions to hang out a few more sheets. The first of these reconnoiter-ing trips was not reassuring. I heard Gerrish say from the other side of the little spruce thicket, " 'Less you keep on the offside of a log when you're limbin' out, you're liable to chop a foot off. Heed what I say." Visions of severed arteries crossed my mind, as I burst through the bushes. Gerrish straightened up. "I'm keepin' a snug watch on him," he said placidly. "He ain't goin' to learn to handle an ax any younger." So monumental was his calm that unreasonably, perhaps, I was convinced.

Fifteen minutes later the air was rent with howls. The worst, I knew as I flew out of the house, had happened. I was no better than a murderess, and what was Ralph going to say to me when he found out how I'd neglected our child?

The scene in the clearing made me mad. No one likes to go through a minor hell over nothing. And it was nothing. Rufus was sitting on a log with a splintered ax handle in his hand, crying at the top of his lungs. Gerrish was squat-ting opposite him, smoking his pipe. I was too furious to speak. I just stood there giving off sparks.

Gerrish looked at me and took his pipe from his mouth. "The young one's got a notion in his head," he said com-fortably, "and if it works, it'll be a real handy thing to know. Seems he's got an idee that bawlin' will fix that there ax shaft. I cal'late we've give it a fair try, but if he ain't dis-couraged, I ain't. Any time he wants to give up and try something else, I'm willin'; only 't seems like an awful waste of energy if bawlin' will do it."

Rufus and I both looked at him and we both saw the same thing, a man absorbed in a problem—and whether the problem concerned a broken ax or the futility of tears made little difference, since either can be serious. I think it was in that moment that we both gave him our trust. Rufus wiped his eyes on the heel of his hand and asked briskly, "What tools you want me to get from Dad?" And that was that, except that right then I lost my baby. He became Gerrish's right-hand man.

Being Gerrish's right-hand man was no sinecure. It not only involved learning to use an ax and a saw and a cant dog, and how to bait and set a rattrap, and not to cry over spilled milk or skinned knees; it required as well the adoption of a whole ethical code.

"What are you doing here?" I asked one day when I came across my son sitting on a rock with his chin in his hands. I'd come to accept, by then, the fact that where Gerrish was, there was Rufus. "Why don't you go play with Gerrish?"

"We don't play," he said with dignity. "We work."

"Excuse me," I apologized, and I was not being ironic. Self-respect assailed, deserves apology. "Why aren't you out working with him?"

"He and Dad are looking for old boom logs and they won't let me in a canoe till I can swim. Gerrish is going to teach me Sunday."

"Can't he teach you to-day?"

He looked at me scornfully: "Dad's paying Gerrish to work weekdays. We can't swim on Dad's time. That's stealing. Gerrish says so." It was as simple as that, the difference between right and wrong, honesty and dishonesty;

and although I could think of several ways to speed Sunday's arrival—starting with appealing to Ralph to give Gerrish the afternoon off and ending with teaching Rufus myself—I said nothing. All I could offer, after all, was privilege or compromise. To exchange either for integrity would have been stealing, too.

I never knew a person who balanced so well the ledger of his living. Most people are meticulous in paying dollar-and-cent debts. To Gerrish, money was only one form of currency and no more important or valid than time or consideration. Once I came across him struggling to mend a pair of choppers—the leather-covers woodsmen wear to protect their woolen mittens from wet and rough usage. I'm a chopper-mender from way back and once bought myself a sailmakers' palm and kit for that very purpose. So I said, "Here, give me that. I can do it in the time it takes you to think about it." He relinquished them without a struggle and thanked me very nicely when the job was done. But the next morning when I came down to cook breakfast, the kitchen floor was scrubbed as white as bone, and almost dry.

"Heavens," I said, "you must have been up before daylight to get this chore done. You don't have to do my work too, you know—not but what I'm grateful."

He smiled his little lopsided smile. "I know you don't relish scrubbin' a floor, and you done me a favor yesterday."

We live in a logging country, and one of the big events of the year is the spring drive. Then the pulpwood which has been cut during the winter is floated down the chain of lakes, sometimes as much as fifty or sixty miles, to the mills across the line in New Hampshire. Our days and nights are filled with the hollow thudding of log upon log as a boom is released through the dam just above us, and goes plunging over the rapids down toward Umbagog. This is our holiday, not because of the drive itself, but because of the wonderful fishing which accompanies it. In normal times we fish only in the early morning and the evening, when the sun is low and the trout and salmon come out from their lurking places in deep holes or under sunken boulders. But during the drive, they follow the booms down the lakes, hiding in the shadow of the close-packed logs and feeding off the grubs that drop from the rotting bark. Some of the fish go down through the dam with the boom, of course; but dozens are caught above the gates, which are closed at the end of each sluicing. The man who gets there quickly, before the fish return to deep water, is due for a half-hour's superb fishing. There is nothing so thrilling to the bred-in-the-bone fly-fisherman as the powerful rush and clean accuracy of a five-pound salmon surging up from the green depths to take a Whitney B Pond or a Parmachene Belle. And we were bone-bred fishermen.

Therefore we had the following arrangement. Since the dam can be plainly seen from the living-room windows, I, whose duties kept me in the house, acted as a sort of Sister Anne. The minute I saw the crew go out onto the walkway to lower the sluice gates, I beat on the gong, and we all dropped whatever we were doing and high-tailed it for the dam. It's wonderful up there in the spring, with the sun shining warm and bright and the wind crisping the clear water. The air smells of cut spruce and of the old snow lying back in the deep woods and of flowering shadbush and the quickening earth. It's as good as a trip to Bermuda, and that's what we considered it—our vacation, our time to howl.

But not so Gerrish. The Sunday after the drive went on down-river and left us to our old ways, he said to Ralph, "What you want I should tackle to-day?"

Ralph gaped. "To-day's Sunday. You lost track of time?"

"Nope. I owe you eighteen hours' work, time I spent fishin'. Figured I'd make it up the next few Sundays." And nothing we said could change him. An upright man does not sell out his birthright of honor for eighteen hours of good fishing.

We had a Siberian husky at that time, Cookie, and the bond between her and Rufus was the bond that exists between every small boy and his dog the world over. She was expecting her first litter, and as time went on, it became increasingly apparent that things were not as they should be. She whimpered in her sleep and lay for long hours panting, her eyes wide and glazed. She refused food and grew thin and shabby. She who had always been high headed and proud clung to us humbly, begging for the comfort which we could not give. Then one morning she howled dismally and ran into a dark corner of the tool shed, where she crouched trembling.

Gerrish looked at her and shook his head. "She ain't right. I helped out for a vet once, a spell back. Seems like I could rec'lect enough so's if you was a-mind to leave us alone——"

That was a long morning. Rufus spent it huddled on the shed steps, sobbing miserably whenever Cookie howled. I tried to induce him to come into the house and help me, but he only looked at me numbly and shook his head, and I could not find the right and simple words to make birth with all its agonies and recompenses a good and natural thing to a little boy. He was too young to be going through this particular gethsemane, I knew, but I was powerless against life.

Then the shed door opened and Gerrish squatted on his heels beside the child. "I got to have some help. S'pose you could lend me a hand? I got to have a feller to hold Cookie's head in his lap and not bawl. Bawlin' would make her nervous. S'pose you could do it?"

I started to protest as Rufus scrambled to his feet, but Gerrish silenced me. "Things are comin' along all right now," he said. "I cal'late there ain't nothin' worse'n sittin' around idle, listenin' to her howl, imaginin' things. A young one can get some desperate wrong notions in his head. Only sure way of shakin' them loose is show him the truth. There's somethin' to be said for the truth. Leastwise, 'tain't nothin' to be ashamed or scared of."

Half an hour later Rufus bustled into the house. I never saw so radiant a face. "We got four pups," he announced importantly. "Mom, you know about dogs having pups? It's——" He sought the right word and proudly produced his newest one. "It's *interesting*!"

There's something to be said for the truth, after all.

Ralph was a man in whose scheme of things makeshift had no place. My slipshod, *laisser-aller* methods were a source of real pain to him. He fumed to Gerrish when I propped up a burned-out grate with a brick, or employed the back of a Stillson wrench to drive a nail, or mended a leaky pan with adhesive tape. There was a right way to do things, and there was no reason why I shouldn't do them that way.

"Wal, she's a woman," Gerrish explained.

"Well, she doesn't have to act like a goddam woman," Ralph retorted.

Then came the day when I fixed the radio. It stopped working right when I wanted to listen to it, so I fixed it. I reached over in back, fanned my fingers blindly about in what felt like a tangle of wires, and music poured out mellowly into the room. I was pretty smug as I reported my success. No, of course I didn't know what ailed the thing. I didn't care. It was working now. What more could anyone ask?

"Oh my God!" Ralph ejaculated with a notable lack of reverence. "Of all the——!" He turned to Gerrish. "Did you ever hear of anything so—so——"

"Not 'zactly." Gerrish was judicial. "My oldest girl fixed a Model T with chewing gum once, though." He chuckled. "Always tickles me to see a woman flub 'round. They're a real ingenious species, in a hen-headed way. Let 'em alone, you're likely to learn some real surprisin' things. Ever see a woman shell peas in a clothes wringer?"

"I've seen Louise open jars in the door hinge, and I must say it didn't tickle me much. We do own pliers."

But a week later I heard him laughing with Gerrish. "Now I've seen everything. You know Louise's latest? She repaired the pump with a bobby pin, and the damn thing runs like a clock. Women! I'm afraid there's nothing to be done about them." And after that he stopped trying.

He eventually arrived at the same conclusion about the weather. I know perfectly well that there is nothing more annoying than to get an outdoor job half done and then have to lay off for three days of rain. The first time that happened after Gerrish came to work for us, Ralph went into his usual routine of pacing the floor, peering out of windows for a break in the clouds, and muttering imprecations. I could hear Gerrish puttering around in the wood-shed, and after a while he came in.

"I got the saws all filed," he said humbly. "They been needin' it, and I been waitin' for a good rainy day. If you was a-mind, I could turn the grindstone and we could get the axes in shape. Then if she don't clear this afternoon, we could put in that shorin' under the kitchen. Nothin' like a good spell of weather to get caught up with ourselves. Feel sort of smart, come the end of a storm, lookin' back at the chores I've got through. Feel like I'd spited the weather."

We never had rainy day trouble after that. As Gerrish once remarked—when we were discussing the possibility of man's eventually being able to control it—weather is all in the mind. If you don't care if it's raining, it isn't raining. Man can manage weather, each to his own ends.

I think perhaps in this attitude lay the index to Gerrish's whole character as I learned to know it in the years that it took really to know a man so quiet and unassuming. In the end I knew him for what he was—the wealthiest man in the world, if wealth is to be reduced to its final term of power. He had a job, the clothes in which he stood, and complete control over weather and time and space and circumstance. A hundred years were nothing to him. I remember one day well, when he and I were paddling the eight miles to Upper Dam, to pick blueberries. The little white half-moons of beach, the rocky points slipping past, the hazy summit of Mount Washington climbing into the sky a state away, were old and familiar to us. We'd been this way so many times before.

But out of a silence he said, "Right over there ain't a

bad site. Good game country and easy defended against the Indians. Plenty of hardwood handy, too."

"Only thing is," I told him, "there's not much level ground for a garden or pasturage"; because suddenly we weren't the boss's wife and the hired hand going about a routine chore. I can't explain it, but it is true that we were the first white men—bearded, ragged, alert—ever to lay eyes upon this lonely, lovely country. We weren't just amusing ourselves with a childish make-believe. Around the next point lay who knew what? Death, perhaps, by ambush; or the wide and gracious interval of natural meadow and noble grove in which we would live out long lives, building, spending our strength and our years in the taming of a harsh and beautiful land to our service. The known ledges, the recognized shore line—all that was familiar and stale—took on a freshness and the beauty of the strange; and life itself was wonderfully rich and new. It was with an almost physical shock that I came back—when the west landing of the Upper Dam carry came into view around a final tongue of land—to the blueberry bucket at my feet where had been a long rifle and a blanket roll; came back to my own time and my own self.

In a sense I have never come back entirely. Never again will the world be an accustomed place to me, nor men of the past or the future, creatures divorced from the now. Time and space—what are they? Nothing but the element in which generation after generation works out the final cumulative destiny.

I don't know how I can make you understand the relationship between Gerrish and me. I loved him, as a child loves her father, as a child loves another child—a love complete and sexless. He was like my own father, who is the gentlest, most understanding man who ever lived. He was like the kid next door, with whom I stole apples and snow-balled cats. We understood each other.

I remember, one time, a guest of ours said to me within his hearing, when I was coping with some household problem in my accustomed fashion, "You know, Louise, you're rather efficient in an unorganized way." That didn't bother me. I know most of my own failings. But it did bother Gerrish, apparently. An hour later I went out into the kitchen and there sat Gerrish, smoking his pipe, rocking like mad, and thinking. "You know, Louise," he said, "*she's* rather inefficient in a well-organized way."

That seemed to me a neat bit of phrase-turning and a touching exhibition of loyalty; but when I came to think it over, it was more than that. It was true. Don't you know people like that yourself, who organize like crazy but never get much done?

I remember once in the late fall when the night air was sharp with the promise of frost and we had a huge fire roar-ing in the fireplace. I got up from where I was sitting, read-ing and eating apples, to look out of the window into the dark—and saw a tree burning outside. Flame curled up from under each feathery limb, leaping red and beautiful, but the tree was not consumed. "Oh, look!" I cried.

Ralph came to gaze over my shoulder. "You dope," he said. "It's only the reflection in the window glass of the fireplace."

I knew that, but to me it was a marvelous and lovely sight.

Gerrish looked over my shoulder, too, and stood silent for a long moment. "Now I know how Moses felt in the desert," he said. "It's agin nature to see a bush burn and not burn. But God! Ain't it pretty!" He had a heart ready to accept miracles, and unless you have a heart like that, miracles don't happen to you.

One thing Gerrish could never understand was psychoanalysis. That was a thing that had never entered his ken until he heard some of my guests and me discussing it one evening. Next morning, when he and I were in complete and sole possession of the kitchen, he said to me, "Look, Louise. I know I ain't very bright and I know I ain't had opportunities. But that stuff you was talking about last night—I couldn't make head nor tail out of it. Way they was talking, sounded like it was the answer to everything."

I tried my best to explain, but I guess I did a poor job, hampered as I was by lack of information and lack of conviction.

"You mean nothin' you do is your own fault?" he asked. "You mean you pay a doctor good money to tell you you act like a damn fool on account of your mother was too fond of you? You drink too much because some schoolteacher laughed at you for making a mistake forty years ago? I dunno, Louise. All them people got more brains than me, but it don't seem sensible. It must be an awful comfortable feelin' that whatever you do, someone else is to blame; but me—wal, I guess I'd ruther take my own blame."

And I guess I would, too, now that it's been pointed out to me. And if some psychiatrist cares to see in this statement a clear case of megalomania or schizophrenia—or whatever the proper terms may be—all right and be damned to him!

I remember the day before Gerrish died. We'd been planting some little apple trees, for, as he said, "You like to leave something for your grandchildren to remember you by.

Happens you can't leave them a million dollars, and I don't know nothin' they'd get more comfort out of than a good-bearin' Northern Spy." We were sitting on the porch overlooking the river—Ralph and Gerrish and I—and the setting sun was in our faces and our ears were full of the lovely sound of water rushing over stone.

"God, but I'm glad I'm me," Gerrish said, "sittin' right here this minute. I been lucky all my life. I can't never remember wishin' I was someone else or someplace else. I been lucky. Ain't many been as lucky as I been."

And I knew that he was right. Not many are lucky enough to have such a love of living, such a palate for life, that merely existing, no matter when or where, is as much as a man can bear for the sheer miraculous joy of it. That kind of luck is given to no one; and few are wise enough to win it.

The next day he went Out on his annual vacation, and less than twenty hours later his daughter Catherine called me up to tell me that he was dead. He died as he had lived, causing the least possible trouble to anyone. His eager heart simply stopped beating. I couldn't believe it, even while I was telling Catherine that, of course, Ralph and I would come to the funeral and, of course, Ralph would act as one of the pallbearers. I couldn't believe it.

I have been to very few funerals in my life. I don't know whether his funeral was a good one or not, because I don't know what a funeral is supposed to be like. I've always thought the whole idea was barbaric and I still think so.

There he lay, a man whom I had never seen, in all the years I knew him, except dressed in rough woods clothes with a disreputable old felt hat pulled down over one eye. Now he wore a neat, blue serge suit and a necktie, and his graying hair was parted neatly. I didn't know him until I saw his hands quietly folded, at last, but bearing still across the knuckles the scar of a burn he had received the week before while he was helping me take a heavy roaster out of the oven. I knew those hands; I knew them well. They were the hands that had cut cord after cord of wood for us, that had been laid in comfort upon my children when they were hurt, that had helped me into boats and onto roofs, had picked berries and tied flies and washed my dishes, through the years. They were the only part of him that was left familiar to me, and they broke my heart.

I thought, "Oh, Gerrish! You don't belong here! You wouldn't like it—you who were always so shy and diffident —you wouldn't like being the center of attention. You'd be so embarrassed. Let's get out of here!"

And suddenly we were out of there. All through the singing and the talking and the weeping and the smell of flowers, we were out of there. We were over at B Pond, watching the gulls inscribe their slow and shining signatures upon a fair clear sky. We were fishing at the Head-of-the-Pond, with a fresh wind nipping across the water which had been ice-free for only a day, shouting to each other—"Lead him away from there! If he ever gets under that boom, we'll lose him sure as shooting!"—as a great salmon leaped at the end of a taut line. He was saying to me, as I fell off a rock into the water in my efforts to net the fish, "Lord, Louise, you *are* a gawm!" We were crossing the ice on the big lake in a snowstorm, hauling at the rope of a handsled, our breaths freezing on the upturned collars of our sheepskins; and we were paddling down the Magalloway in the breathless and blistering heat of an August noon. We were swimming the river, climbing the ridges, walking the trails that we both knew so well. We were sitting on the back steps in the cool of the evening after a hard, hot day, smoking and talking quietly. His body lay there in state, with the flowers banked about it and the music rolling over it in muted waves; but he wasn't there. He was in all the places we had loved, he and Ralph and I, where the flowers are shy and scentless and the music of wind and water is wild and free.

They buried him on a hillside that overlooked a little lake. It was a nice place to be buried. Four men for whom he had worked during his life carried him there on their shoulders. He'd done so much for them in life—Ralph and the other three—and it seemed to me fitting that in the end they should do this one final service for him. He would have liked it if he could have known. He'd have been pleased and touched, although he would have said, "No need for you to put yourselves out for me." He was like that.

It was weeks before I could remember not to set a plate for him at the table. It has been three years, and I still find myself saving things to tell him when he gets in from the woodlot. I'd like to tell him right this minute about a letter I got a few nights ago, from a man named Ed Blodgett.

I don't know Ed Blodgett from a hole in the ground, nor he me; but he'd just read a piece I'd written for *The Reader's Digest* about Gerrish as the most unforgettable character I'd known—so he wrote me. He told me he'd been up on the Aleutians, and he and some fellow engineers had decided to build a rough stone cairn on a nameless little island there. They started it with seventeen stones, one each "for seventeen good guys who had lost their lives there in an unheralded misadventure of this man's war." I'll tell the rest of it in Ed Blodgett's words. He won't mind, I'm sure.

When we put this thing up there and scratched men's names on rocks without benefit of chaplain, we decided that if and when circumstances might allow—well, just to give the thing mass enough to be seen at all—each person of the building squad could at some time or other come in with another simple rock for some home-front person. The only stipulation was that this person had to be made of what it takes.

My own choice in this peculiarly sentimental little matter has been delayed; it's hard to name one name when even those faces in the legitimate Hall of Fame must have gotten there by virtue of a lot of unnamed friendly help along the way. Captain Brooks held off and pawed around for the name of a New Hampshire man to symbolize the support of his own state toward this crazy war. I, in turn, pawed over Maine, and was still at a loss to choose from among a lot of the finest people I have known.

To-day I let you lump-sum my choice—sort of blending all my candidates into a definite composite. I wrote Captain Brooks, "The next time your boat puts in for water, scratch *Gerrish* on a bigger and better rock for me, and let that settle my account."

I like to think of that name there, half a world away, on a cold and lonely North Pacific island. I can't think of a better place for it, there between open sky and open sea, in company with the names of other men who were fine and good and brave. I thank you, Ed Blodgett. I wish I could tell Gerrish about it, when he comes in for supper.

But he won't be coming again for me to tell, although he is still in the house. He is like the air we breathe, the bread we live by, the healing rain. He is like the foundation under us and the rooftree over our heads—things we accept and depend upon, although we cannot see them. We remember and speak of him often, and the things he stood for are a part of our lives. Perhaps a hundred years from now my grandchildren will still be saying his name, handed down to them through my children, when they talk of honesty and integrity.

He was the hired help; and I believe that now, wherever he may be, he at last knows, once and for all, his true place.

CHAPTER III

Our Legal Residence

THE OTHER DAY I got to thinking about Upton and wondering what was happening over there. Although for all practical purposes we live in Unorganized Territory—that is, territory which is wild land under no government except the remote control of the State and the more immediate control of our own good sense or lack of it—technically we are citizens of Upton. The back line of the town passes half a mile north of us, so we are Organized. We have no roads except the short carry that connects the two lakes between which we live—and that's more of a dry gulch than a road— no fire or police protection except the State warden services, no telephone except a private lumber-camp line, no light or power except kerosene lamps and gasoline motors, and no community life except the casual and unplanned assembling in someone's kitchen, or on someone's boat landing, of various members of the three families who live in this neck of the woods. But we vote, register births, deaths, cars, and dogs, and pay taxes in Upton. That's Organization.

The center of the village lies to the south of us beyond swamp and blowdown and stream and forest, nine miles as the crow flies. We're not crows, so we seldom get over there except for the annual Town Meeting, come the first Mon-

58

day in March. Nevertheless the town fascinates me, and every now and then I have to check up on it.

There was a time, so they tell me, when Upton was a thriving and prosperous community, sufficient unto its own needs. Nothing was sold in stores except coffee, tea, salt, spices, tobacco, hardware, and the few other items that a New Englander cannot grow or contrive. Everybody farmed, and every farm supported itself. Where now the neglected fields are springing up to brush, wheat rippled golden in the breeze, and the orchards, where now only the deer feed on the tired old trees' paltry fruit, were bountiful and well tended. And that's not all. The town was as independent of the world outside for its social life as it was for material things. There were dances and church socials and school and Grange affairs. Nobody went anywhere outside of town, except on rare and special occasions. Why should he? Everything anyone wanted or needed was to be had at home.

Upton isn't like that now. When first I came to this country, there still remained some semblance of the old days. The population of the town then was 185 persons, and on Saturday nights there were still dances and box suppers, attended by the citizens and the lumberjacks for miles around.

Do you know about box suppers? They are quite a rig. The girls and women put up lunches for two in boxes and wrap them up as spectacularly as possible. Most married women are content with colored paper and splashing bows and evergreen sprigs. They know that their own husbands will buy their boxes. But the young girls really go to town. I remember seeing one box which was camouflaged with roofing paper to look like a jagged reef. Pounding surf was painted about its base and on the top was a toy lighthouse with a flashlight inside, so that it really shone. That was something! It sold at auction for five dollars to a sawyer from Barnett's Number Three Camp.

The boxes are smuggled into the hall and placed surreptitiously on the platform. At suppertime, the auctioneer, who may be the minister or the First Selectman, sells them off to the highest bidder, who buys the girl along with the box, so to speak. In other words, if a man buys your box, you eat supper out of it with him and he is your escort for the rest of the evening. Naturally, if you are engaged to a man, or even merely doing what is locally known as "settin' up nights" with him, it's all right to give him an advance viewing of your masterpiece, so that he won't get stuck, through misunderstanding, with the blonde hussy out Surplus way who's been chasing him for the last six months. That's only sensible. But if you're foot-loose and fancy-free, with an eye on the tall, dark straw boss from the C Pond operation—well, a box supper is your chance to do some spadework with ingenious decorations and superb chocolate cake.

When Whit Roberts and Doc Stuart, two men in their middle-sixties who work for me summers, get to talking about the old days and the fun they used to have about their home town of Andover—our postal address—they sooner or later get on the subject of dances. A dance, it seems, was an inferior and spiritless affair unless at least one good fight occurred. The bigger the fight, the better the dance. They agree that the best dance they ever had in Andover was the one where a crowd from Rumford showed up, in a condition described as well shellacked, and tried to stop festivities. Andover rallied its forces and the dance floor, which is on the second story of the Town Hall, became the scene of a free-for-all. Two Andover men stood at the door and two more at the head of the stairs. As soon as one of the enemy was anywhere near *hors de combat,* he was handed over to the first pair, who passed him to the second pair, who flung him down the length of the flight. "We sure cleaned up that cat-hop in jig-time," Doc recalls gleefully. "Remember that big galoot, Whit? He never touched bottom till the first landing. I thought to Christ the side of the building was going to cave when he lit. That was one good dance!"

The Upton dances, when I knew them, were considerably more peaceable. The only fight I ever knew about—except for private, behind-the-hall fights—occurred when a lumberjack named Felix King was so ill advised as to take a drink out of a bottle of rum in the middle of the dance floor. Now I know Felix King. For all he used to be a professional prize fighter, he's no troublemaker. He just didn't understand that this was a genteel gathering. He told me the next day that if the constable had asked him nicely to go outside and do his drinking, he would have apologized and gone. Instead, the constable, who is a rabid teetotaler, picked up a folding chair and smashed it over Felix's head. The fight was on.

Buster Williamson, a young guide whom I have known almost since he was in three-cornered pants, gave me his version of it. "I jumped in on Felix's side," he related in his moderate voice. "I'd ought to have stuck by the home-town boys; but you know, if there's anything in the world I just can't stand to see, it's someone getting a chair broke over his head. Always gets my dander up." How's that for a man of delicate sensibilities? I felt proud of Buster. He went on, " 'Twould have been all over in a minute, only Albert Judkin turned out all the lights. Crimey, you couldn't tell who was hitting who, nor where the next sock on your own jaw was comin' from. She was pretty confused there for a minute."

I was pretty confused, too. "Why'd he turn the lights out?"

"Too many movies and western stories. You know how it is in a border-town saloon." I assured him, falsely, that I did. "The minute gunplay starts, someone shoots out the lights. That's sensible, when lead's a-flyin'. But when it's just a little old ordinary fistfight—"

I could see Buster's point, but I could also sympathize with Albert. When life holds as few chances for playing man of action as most of our lives hold, the temptation to act dramatically when the rare opportunity offers is overpowering. I dramatize myself half the time, for my own entertainment. I didn't blame Albert. I'm happy to report that he's been in the Air Corps for two years now and loves it. He doesn't have to be content now with synthetic action and adventure.

They don't have dances and box suppers now in Upton. The population now is forty-eight, even counting the members of the Rich household, who are after all only common-law citizens. The town is dying, and I want to know why. The people in Upton with whom I have talked insist that it is the war, that men have been forced to leave town to go into the services—which is true—and that others have chosen to leave for the high wages of the shipyards of Bath and Brunswick and South Portland. That's true, too. They'll be back, everyone says. This is only a temporary slump. That, I think, is not true. The decline set in long before the war was ever thought of, and while there will be some migration back, Upton will never be again what once it was.

Why? For a while I thought it was because of the automobile. A horse-and-buggy-civilization·adherent from way back, I blame everything I possibly can on the automobile, its first cousin the airplane, its grand-nephew the outboard motor, and while I'm at it, the movie and the push-button home. Anybody with half a brain can argue me down. My position is untenable, I know. I'm full of prejudice, misinformation, and unprogressiveness. But I still feel that mere speed and motion are not necessarily progress, and I'd still like to know what people are going to do with the time they save by using electric dishwashers. Unless it's something pretty rewarding, they'd better do their dishes by hand and learn to like it. I believe that progress is a thing of mind, heart, and attitude rather than of mechanical efficiency, and that a philosophy that includes manual labor as good is in advance of one that rejects it as bad. But I'm self-admittedly a crackpot on this subject.

In the case of Upton, however, I'm afraid I can't wholly blame the gasoline motor. I've about decided that there is a moral question involved here. In its heyday the town depended upon two things for its prosperity, farming and lumbering. It took, in short, what the earth had to give; but, first in lumbering, later in farming, it tried to cheat the earth. The woods were slashed, and there has been no attempt at reforestation. The woods will grow up again, eventually, of their own accord; but it will be a long time before there are any lumbering operations of any importance around Upton and the town is suffering and will continue to suffer.

The attempt to cheat the earth started later in farming. People used to tend their farms religiously, putting time and thought and labor back into the ground for the things they took out. There are still individual farmers who do so,

of course, in Upton as elsewhere, and they're getting along
all right. But a common attitude arose that it was more fun
to slat through the milking of one cow, jump into the jalopy
and hare off to Berlin (N. H.) to the movies, stopping en
route at the A&P for butter, than it was to milk four cows,
shovel the manure back into the ground, and make your
own butter. You just can't do business with the land that
way.

There are three ways to get into Upton from here, and
every one of them is possessed of such beauty that I'm never
able to decide which way I like best. There is no comparison
possible, since each way differs from the others in all re-
spects. The way we used to go to Town Meeting was the
shortest, hardest way—through the woods on snowshoes. It's
also the least spectacular way. But there is one part of the
journey that pays for all the rest of the struggle through
swamp and slash, and that is the stretch across the top of B
Pond Ridge.

When you go across B Pond Ridge in the summer, it's just
another piece of woods, leafy and green and closed in. The
trail is rough and wet and narrow between the boulders, and
you have to watch your footing and the spots on the trees
closely. In this country we don't blaze a trail; we spot it out,
but it means the same thing—putting ax or paint marks on
trees at about eye level, to mark the way. Most of the trees
on top of the Ridge are hardwood—yellow and white birch,
maple, and beech—with comparatively little black growth—
fir, spruce, and pine—mingled with it.

And that is what gives B Pond Ridge its special character
in winter. You climb up the slope through the tunnels of
the black growth and come suddenly out into a high, open,

airy space. The four-foot-deep snow is level and unmarked
between the trunks of the trees, and the spots, which should
be at eye level, are below the knee. It's odd to look down
to see them, and it's odd to look up and see, instead of a
roof of green plumes, the open, silky, twig-fretted sky. The
maples and birches are bare, beautiful and clean with the
clean beauty of all skeletons; but the beeches still hold their
leaves, faded now from red-veined green to a light gold.
Their boles and branches are a pale silver. Perhaps it's
looking down to see the spots that does it; perhaps it's seeing the sky so near; or perhaps it's the breathing space all
around. Whatever it is, you feel like a giant in a vast cere-
monial place of crystal and silver and gold. It's a place that
you cannot defile with your own petty, personal problems.
So you walk, godlike and free, for a few moments out of
time. Then the land dips down, you plunge again into the
shadow of the evergreens, and so come back, brushed with
immortality, to mortal life and mortal living.

The second way to get to Upton from here is through
Grafton Notch. This involves a trip all around Robin
Hood's barn. To get to a place nine miles from your starting point, you travel over fifty miles by boat or snowmobile
and car. I became very familiar with this route the winter
we rented a house in Upton, and installed my Catherine
Jacobs in it to tend the children, so Rufus could go to
school. The reason we went by Grafton Notch instead of
through the woods was that there was always something like
a high chair or six cases of canned milk or twelve extra
blankets which had to be delivered at the Upton house, and
we never felt quite up to toting them on our backs across
the Ridge. So we'd corral Larry Parsons in a good mood—
and in fairness I must say that 99.6 per cent of his moods

are good (that's his trouble)—and pin him down to what day would be most convenient for him to drive us over. We'd go to Rumford, pick up some delicacies for Catherine—the General Store in Upton usually doesn't run to such exotic fare as lettuce or celery—and set off by the Bethel road.

I don't know—I really do not know—whether it's the topography of the Notch or what little I know of its history that so impresses me. After you leave Newry you look ahead and see a great cleft in the wall of mountains to the west, and you know that you must enter and pass through that forbidding gate. The road climbs beside a noisy stream, and soon your ears begin to ring. Farms fall behind and below and there is nothing but woods and the rush of water and mountainsides that come closer and closer. Then you start seeing them—the abandoned fields, the gaping cellar holes, the weary orchards that line the road in the shadow of the towering outcroppings of rock that are the Notch.

How can I make you see and feel those lofty ledges, imponderable against the sky? They always shine, being always wet or glazed with ice, for somehow, from the bowels of the earth, springs leap to the mountaintop and perpetually water the infertile rock. They are cold, those ledges, and implacable, the sworn enemies of anything warm and human and vulnerable. Seeing them, feeling their weight upon the spirit, you understand why no one any longer lives in Grafton Notch.

For people once lived there. Grafton Notch was once the Town of Grafton, holding a charter, incorporated under the State. Those people must have worked hard. No farmer, especially in New England and, more especially, under pioneering conditions, has an easy life. But here it was no use. Everything was against them. Even the seasons betrayed them. There is never a month in the year, not even July or August, that doesn't bring a black killing frost to Grafton Notch. So they gave up and moved away, one by one, until the handful left held a meeting and voted to return the charter to the State. I cannot imagine a more heartbreaking thing than to have given up publicly, by common consent, the enterprise upon which they must have embarked with such high hearts, to have given up years of labor, the visions of comfortable homes, the dreams of long futures for their children and their grandchildren on the land which they had believed needed only courage and patience and strength to tame.

That's the accepted reason why the Town of Grafton was abandoned. But I never go through the Notch without wondering what really happened to the people who lived there in the years before they finally gave up. That foundation work there, so close under the shoulder of the mountain that the sun shines into it only briefly at noon, once supported a house. What happened in that house, long ago? Did the woman rise day after day and stare out of her sunless window at the dark hulk of the mountain until at last it became more than a mountain? Did she think, "I mustn't look! I must not look!"—and busy herself with household chores, inventing tasks, afraid to stop, knowing hopelessly that the mountain could wait, that it was in no hurry, that sooner or later it would cut off the light of sanity as it cut off the light of the sun? What happened on the day when her husband came in from the fields and found her gone and in her place a witless, mumbling stranger? I don't know. I don't know that anything like that happened at all—but the whole feel of the place is evil.

And what about the little graveyard back on a knoll? I

know who is buried there—nine children of one family. They all died within a week of what was called "black diphtheria." That I know. What I don't know is how the parents bore a thing like that. Were they mercifully shocked into numbness? Or was each death a further refinement of torture, with the sadistic mountain smiling on? How can one know a thing like that? How can one begin to imagine it?

What about the woman who refused to leave the Notch? She was alive when first I came here—an old, old woman living all alone in a great empty house. The lumber company that bought up all the land about there tried to buy her farm, but she refused to leave for any amount of money. I never saw her and now she is dead, but I thought about her often and I still think about her. Why did she stay? Did she love the place? Or was she determined that her dust should mingle, in the end, with the dust of someone who meant more to her—through either love or hate—than anything life elsewhere could offer her? Or was she just plain stubborn, determined no mountain should get the best of her? What did she think about on winter nights when the wind screamed off the mountain and the Notch was choked with driven snow, as she peered out into blackness, her veined old hand shielding her eyes against her lamp's glare upon the pane, and remembered the dozen lights that once answered the gleam of her own? I used to think about her lamp, one tiny spark of light in all that dark. It's out, now. There's nothing now but dark in all the Notch.

I said the Notch was beautiful, and it is beautiful—but with a savage sinister beauty. I'm always glad to leave it behind and come out onto the flat that leads into Upton.

The third way to reach Upton from here is by way of Umbagog, and I guess that's the way I really like best, be-

cause I'd rather go to hell in a boat than to heaven by any
other means of transportation. I simply *love* boats in spite
of all the grief they've caused me, first and last. We have on
Umbagog (pronounced with the accent on the second syl-
lable, *bay*) a twenty-eight-foot, slow old Tappon cabin
cruiser with a Kermath motor, named *Puss*. The *Puss* is my
boat, since I don't mind mogging along at eight miles an
hour, watching the scenery go by. Such leisurely progress
drove Ralph nuts, so his boat was a Chris-craft with an 85 h.p.
motor, in which he tore about at practically the speed of
light. It's name was *Igliffe,* the French attempt, as you probably know, at "High Life." The *Igliffe* was definitely High
Life as far as the Riches are concerned. We just aren't that
stylish; and Holy Moses, how I hated that boat! On the
occasions when I couldn't possibly get out of riding in it, I
sat with cold sweat running down my spine, my fingers
crossed, and a prayer in my heart that the insurance would
cover the children's education. This was not plain sissy. I've
had a history of bitter experiences in that damn Chris-craft.
I'll tell you about them sometime.

In order to get to Upton center from here by way of Umbagog, you cover a distance of sixteen miles and pass through
four townships and two states. You start out in Upton,
Maine, and drive three and a half miles to Sunday Cove,
which is in Magalloway Plantation (still Maine); there you
embark, if you're lucky, on the *Puss*. If your luck is out,
that's the day you're using the Chris-craft. A third of the
way down Umbagog's twelve-mile length, you line yourself
up with the third pumpkin pine of seven on a ridge on the
west shore and a rock on Tyler Point on the east shore.
Then you know you are in Errol, New Hampshire, and if
you've been trolling off the stern, you reel in, because the

New Hampshire game warden has a short way with Maini-
acs fishing in his waters. You stay in Errol for about six
miles, navigate a narrow gut marked by a buoy, turn sharp
west, then sharp east in front of Jessie Potter's farm, and
you are in the unorganized township of Cambridge, New
Hampshire, for a short time. When you pass Lakeside—there
used to be a hotel there once, but now there is only a clearing and an abandoned sawmill—you're back in Upton again,
although by no means at the center. You still have to walk
a mile up a hill as steep as the side of a barn, and usually
Ralph and I had to horse not only ourselves, but our infant
Dinah slung between us in a clothesbasket as well, up what
he called "that Christly damn mountain."

The feature about this approach that's so lovely is that
about halfway down the lake you begin to see the town. Upton is the highest civic center in Maine, smack on the top
of a hill, and it looks, from the lake, exactly like a toy village, with tiny houses spaced along ribbons of road, the
church and school neat in the center, and a doll's patchwork
quilt of fields spread out about it. It looks sweet. It looks
as if elves lived there and busied themselves with good deeds,
which is actually far from the truth.

The truth is, of course, that people live there and busy
themselves with the occupation of living, which includes
inevitably deeds both good and bad. My better sense—which
probably isn't Grade A—tells me that people everywhere are
about the same, taken by and large. A few are vicious, a few
are saintly, but the large majority are neither—or a combination of both, which means the same thing. Unquestion-
ably the people of Upton are like that, too, only something
—either the elfin appearance of the village from the lake, or
the necessity of passing through beauty to get there, no mat-

ter how you go, or the fact that I am not in town often
enough to hear anything but the highlights of its activities
—so biases my judgment that everything Uptonians say or
do takes on a special and unearthly significance.

Any human behavior short of the epic is incongruous in
Upton. The whole world spreads out below and around it,
so wide and lovely that you can't believe it's true. You can
see all of Umbagog like a living map, with the dark stains
where cat's-paws of wind roughen the surface, appearing
and fading. Standing in sunlight, you can see a thunderstorm roll down the narrow Magalloway Valley, ten miles
away, the black boil of cloud laced with lightning. Having
been along the Magalloway in a storm, you know what a
tumult of howling wind and slashing rain and falling trees
rages there; but, where you stand, birds sing in the quiet
and daisies nod gently in peaceful meadows. Or on a fall
morning, looking southwest through the bland hazy air, you
see glittering peaks of snow rearing above the flame of
autumn forests. The background is for colossal deeds of self-
abnegation, for Greek tragedy, for deathless acts of bravery
and love. There is no place here for meanness; no one would
have the heart, you think, for smallness and spite.

But you'd be wrong. I went over to Upton one spring
when Rufus was boarding at the Allens' and found myself
involved in the bitterest and most futile war in history—
even granting that in my book all war is futile. A bitter war
has more to be said for it than a polite one, as far as I am
concerned. I know that the popular attitude is against total
war, but to me total war is the only war that makes sense.

The War of the Grain Sacks was a total war. It seems that
there is a brand of cattle feed that comes in special sacks.
Most grain bags are of unbleached cotton with lettering on

them, and they are all right, after the grain is gone and you have bleached them out, for dish towels. The grain that is sold at the one store in Upton comes in sacks made of cotton prints. There is no advertising matter on them at all and the patterns are very pretty and original. There are all kinds of floral prints, some plaids and checks, and, the one I love best of all, an all-over design of little feathers in red and yellow and blue. Four grain sacks will make the backing for a patchwork quilt, two will make a dress if you're not too portly, and one will curtain a window. So while the grain is being bought primarily to feed the cattle, no woman in Upton is going to let her husband just go up on the Hill and pick up a sack of feed. She goes with him and picks out the sacks with either (a) the print that appeals to her most or (b) the one like the two she has already, so she can make curtains for the three kitchen windows.

It doesn't take much imagination to see that conflict is bound to arise. Three or four women are bound to be collecting the same pattern, and it's bound to be the rare item that occurs only once in about seven truckloads of feed. Then—well!

I, all innocent and full of sweetness and light, arrived in Upton with no inkling of this. I met an acquaintance walking down the road and suggested that we go together to call on Myra. (Myra is just a name I'm using.) She elevated her nose. "*You* can go," she said. "*If* you want to. But *I'm* not on speaking terms with Myra."

I was flabbergasted. I'd thought she and Myra were as close as bark to tree. "Good Lord——" I commenced.

"After what she did to me! Honestly, Louise, I've been good to that woman. Nobody'll ever know—well, all I can say is that some people simply don't know what gratitude and decency mean. I could tell you a thing or two, if I wanted to. I could tell about the times she met a certain party up on Back Street, and her with a good husband not suspecting a thing—but I'm not like that. After all I've done for her, when she knew perfectly well because I told her myself that I had three yellow-daisy grain sacks already and was just waiting to get the fourth to make up my Star of Bethlehem quilt, what does she do but rush up to the store when she sees the grain truck come and buy the only yellow daisy they have, right out from under my face and eyes before they'd ever unloaded the truck. Don't worry, I'll get even. She's collecting morning glories, and I know where there's one she could get. Just as soon as I can get down to the place it's at, I'm going to get it myself and flaunt it in her face—"

There was more—a lot more. I got away as soon as I could, thinking what a shame! It was really too bad that a woman as young as my acquaintance should lose her mind and become obsessed with feed bags.

But I soon found that she was not alone in her obsession. Everywhere I went tales of perfidy and double-dealing poured into my astonished ear. It never stopped with the current offense of hi-jacking a grain sack, either. I think I heard about every family skeleton, or suspected skeleton, of the past fifty years. It was awful. I was glad when it was time for me to go home to the woods, and I dreaded the day when I'd have to go back into that lionesses' den.

But of course when I did go back, two months later, it was all over and forgotten. Everything was peaceful and everybody loved everybody, in the universal pattern of interwar periods.

Who but a Uptonian would give, sincerely and with a

straight face, this reason for not accepting an invitation to come down the road three hundred yards and spend the evening playing Sixty-three, a card game much in vogue in Upton: "Nope, thanks all the same. But I've got my shoes off." And yet I heard with my own ears Jim Barnett, my landlord for the ten months we rented the Upton house, tell his nextdoor neighbor exactly that over the telephone. The obvious retort is, "Well, put them on again." But, in Upton, the fact that you have your shoes off is reason enough for not stirring out of your house until the next day. You don't take your shoes off until you've settled in for the night. You may still stay up for hours, reading, listening to the radio, or just playing with the cat; but once you get your shoes off, you're your own man. Nobody in his right mind is going to try to sell a guy with his shoes off the silly notion that he has a moral or social responsibility in the world until the following sunrise.

In Upton anything can happen. Just about a year ago now I acquired our current cat in Upton, after having called all the gods to witness that I was through with cats. One yard cat, yes, since we have deer mice to contend with and there is nothing better than a good cat to keep them down.

Speaking generally, I don't like rodents, but deer mice are something else again. They are clean, big-eared, ingratiating little devils. If I could have just a pair of them, I would love them dearly. I had one for a pet once. It lived under the eaves. At that time I was going to bed nights before it was "dark under the table," because I was pregnant and got tired at the end of the day. Ralph and Gerrish might sit up and talk until the ungodly hour of nine-thirty, but I retired with a good book as soon as the supper dishes were done. The minute I was comfortably propped up, book in hand, box of saltines at elbow, my little friend, whose name was Abercrombie H. Fitch, would come running along a rafter, skitter down a stud, and join me. We had a lot of fun. He'd sit on the foot of the bed eating cracker crumbs while I read aloud to him. "The world is too much with us, late and soon," I would declaim, and he'd bow his head in contemplation. I've never told a soul about this until now. It really sounds terrible to say of a woman, "Oooo! *She* takes mice to bed with her!" It sounds psychopathic.

But Abercrombie H. Fitch notwithstanding, enough is enough. When the deer-mouse population gets to the point where you have to set the table with a .22 revolver at each place alongside the spoons to insure getting anything to eat, it's time to get a cat.

We had a cat, a handsome gray tiger named, for reasons too complicated to go into now, Carter-Glass-With-Reservations. He was a very special cat. The woman who gave him to me informed me that he was no riffraff. *His* father was summer folks from Boston! So we didn't need another cat. Nevertheless, one fine day when Catherine had gone to the West Coast to see her Marine husband off to the wars and I was perforce in charge of the Upton house complete with her and my assorted children, Rufus came lugging about an ounce of black-and-white kitten into the house.

"Take that right back where you got it," I said firmly.

"But some man on a team gave it to me for my own."

"What man on what team?"

"I don't know. They're sitting over on the store steps."

I took off my apron, put on some lipstick, and crossed the road to the store. An assortment of lumberjacks and river drivers off the Cambridge River drive was draped over the porch.

"Which one of you," I asked coldly, "gave my little boy that cat?"

A handsome Frenchman snatched off his cap. "That is the smartest kitten in the world. We find it with its mother in camp when we go on the drive. We grow to love it. Can we then break camp and leave it perhaps to be eaten by foxes? So we bring it out on the tote team and look for a nice home with good people. Madame, you will never regret——"

"That's all very well," I said. "But you've passed a dozen houses since you came off East B. Why didn't you leave it at one of them?"

"At the first house we knock, the lady comes to the door, screams, and slams again the door. At every other house the answer is 'No,' when we ask 'Do you want a nice kitten?' So we come to your house and see the boy in the yard——"

"And this time you get smart and don't bother to knock and ask," I finished it for him, and I gave him the meanest look at my command. Then I looked at Rufus, hugging his new pet and pleading with his eyes. I didn't want another cat, but still—I made a last effort. "Is it male or female?"

I knew the answer to that already. Of course it was a male. Any cat that someone is trying to give away is always a male. What happens to its sex after you have taken it to your bosom is something else again. It's always a male to start with, and all I needed to steel me to the point of hatefully refusing to accept it was to be given that motheaten old line.

Now this could have happened nowhere but in Upton, I swear. Every man jack there spoke up with one accord: "Lady, we ain't got no idea." What could I do but keep the cat? And I know you're not going to believe this, but it did turn out to be a male. Shortly after that a fox got Carter—foxes love to eat tomcats better than anything, and that is why tomcat meat is used so much for fox bait—so everything worked out perfectly. We named our new cat Cambridge, because he came off the Cambridge drive, although Doc Stuart insists on calling him Mona Letitia Angelbird, in a sugary coo. Doc is slightly foolish over cats. We still have Cambridge and he really is the smartest cat in the world.

Joe Mooney, who is the switchboard operator over at the Brown Farm, always refers to Upton as P. I., Pinnacle, because so many P. I.'s live there. Strictly speaking, a P. I. is one who hails originally from Prince Edward's Island; but around here it has come to be used loosely to refer to any Canadian who isn't a Frenchman. A Canadian Frenchman is just a Frenchman. If you mean a man from France—and you very seldom do—you say a French Frenchman.

Jim Barnett was telling me about an aftermath of the Bemis fire. Bemis was a town up on Mooselucmeguntic which was completely destroyed about forty years ago in what must have been a hideous forest fire. It has never been rebuilt. A guide from Upper Dam was describing the holocaust to his sport, a woman from the city. He told her about the deer and bear and small game running out of the furnace into the lines of fire-fighters, too terrified of the inferno behind to remember to be afraid of man; about houses going up in a flash of flame; about great trees exploding. "But the most pitiful sight," he said, "was a poor damn P. I. that came running out of the woods, with his hair all burned off him and his eyes so swoll shut with smoke he couldn't see a goddamn thing. He came blundering up to us, whimpering and whining——"

His sport was a humane woman. "For heaven's sake," she asked, "why didn't you take a club and put the poor thing out of its misery?"

This tickles Jim, because he's a P. I. himself. "I don't know," he'll add, "but what she had the right idea about P. I.'s at that."

Every year at Town Meeting a dinner is served in Upton as in all small New England towns; and every year the committee solicits food for the meal. The year Catherine was over there with the children, she got braced with the rest of the housewives and her contribution was to be a salad. She decided, understandably, that she'd go all out to make a good one. She was new in the community but she'd lived in small towns all her life and she knew all about the scrutiny and comment to which her donation would be subjected. So instead of turning in the routine potato or cabbage salad, she sent out specially for not only lettuce, but endive, escarole, and what-have-you, for greens. This she arranged about a mold of fruit-filled lime jello on a large platter, and decorated it with squirligigs of mayonnaise. She told me it looked lovely, and I don't doubt for a moment but what it did. What's more, every scrap was eaten.

But the next day one of the committee returned the platter, along with her personal reaction to Catherine's effort. Catherine called me up, via the Brown Farm, to tell me about it, shouting at the top of her lungs, over a very poor circuit, to make me understand. "Hey, Louise. Can you hear me? She said, 'I never see nothing quite like it, outside a magazine picture. It looked pretty. Tasted funny, though. But I guess I could get used to it.' Can you hear me, Louise? What I think is, she'd better be careful. For all she knows, it might be habit forming."

I'll tell you one thing I especially like about Upton, and that is that you don't have to dress up to go to church, although you can if you want to. I remember the Christmas Eve when we all went to the church "Christmas tree." Ralph and I had just come out of the woods to spend the holiday with the children and Catherine, so we had on our woods clothes—ski-pants, mackinaws, and mittens. It didn't make any difference. In front of me sat a woman wearing a silk dress and a fur coat, but the girl who sang the solo, "Silent Night," from beside the great Christmas tree, had on ski-pants, too. The minister, Mr. Scruton, wore a store suit, and so did one other man; but all the rest were dressed in sheepskins and wool pants tucked into gum-boots. I think it's nice to dress up in your best clothes to go to church, as a way of indicating respect for the Lord and His house; but I think it's even nicer to be able to feel that the Lord doesn't really mind what you have on. That was a lovely service in the bare little church, with Mrs. Scruton playing the parlor organ and all of us in our everyday work clothes singing at the top of our lungs "O Little Town of Bethlehem." I never went to a lovelier, not even in the Cathedral of St. John the Divine.

The last time I was in Upton I bought a quart Mason jar of cream from a man who shall remain nameless, for reasons which will be obvious. The cream was so thick that it had to be spooned out of the jar—marvelous gold richness, the like of which I hadn't seen since Pearl Harbor. "Hey!" I said. "Don't you know it's against the law now to sell cream like this? Not that I'm complaining. Perish forbid! But it's still against the rules."

He looked at me levelly and gave his suspenders a hitch. "Mis' Rich, any day any goddamn government can horn into my dairy room and tell *me* how to set my separator and make it stick will be The Day. This is the kind of cream I sell. When I have to stop, I'll shoot my cows and cut my own throat."

I may be fanciful, although I have never thought I was. I may be sentimental, although that was one standard argument between me and Ralph—that I had no sentiment and he had too much. Women, by and large, are realists. The men are the dreamers; and Ralph and I were pretty average, ran pretty true to form. But this I have always thought about Upton: That Tom Paine, writing almost two hundred years ago, meant that town when he inscribed, "When it shall be said, my poor are happy; neither ignorance nor distress is to be found among them; my jails are empty of prisoners, my streets of beggars; the aged are not in want, the taxes are not oppressive; when these things are said, then may that country boast of its government."

That's Upton. Everybody is poor, so nobody minds. Everybody can read and write, and does. Nobody suffers cold or hunger. The jail has fallen in and is slowly being eaten by porcupines. It's been years since it had a tenant. The aged are not in want, since filial responsibility still survives there. The taxes are not oppressive, only large enough to remind one of a civic responsibility. Upton may boast of its government. Its faults are those of human nature, not of political corruption.

Yes, I do like Upton! One of these days I'm going to sweep myself together and get to go over there and check up on the town.

CHAPTER IV

The Whirl Around the Lakes

PEOPLE IN THIS part of country never, never, *never* take canoe trips for the fun of it. They have to spend too much time pushing canoes about on purely business errands to list that particular activity under the heading of pleasure. Let the sports break their silly backs if they want to, shoving those fool things around all day long for no better purpose than to look at the scenery and get a little fresh air. Men of reason know enough to keep the damn rigs in their proper place, which is that of the strictly utilitarian.

After I had lived in this country for eight years, I began to consider myself a native. I talked more or less like a native, dressed more or less like a native, and certainly acted like one. When I meant "Eat your dinner," I was likely as not to say, "Wind it into you." When I cussed, I said, "Jesus to Jesus and nine hands around," or "Jumped-up Jehovah." I wore gumboots in sloppy weather and plaid wool shirts in winter. I could handle an axe or a bucksaw or a cant dog. Only in one respect did the rot of effete civilization resist all attempts at cauterizing: I still had a sneaking desire to take a canoe trip around the thirty-mile circuit of the lakes, a weakness that I managed for a long time to conceal.

But one fine day the whole family plus the Miller family,

equipped with blueberry pails and sandwiches, embarked on the Miller boat to spend a day at Prospect, where the best and biggest blueberries grow. We slid up the calm surface of the Lower Richardson, and passed between Horse-beef and Portland Points into the Narrows, the winding passage that connects the two Richardson lakes. We waved at whatever Pearsons were sitting on their porches, passed Pine Island and commented on the fact that the fire warden didn't seem to be in residence, and then commenced to play our game of pretending that we'd never been this way before. We picked out suitable sites for homesteading, saw deer and bear where there were no deer and bear, and speculated on what lay at the other end of the carry leading up from the dilapidated landing around the last point. We all knew perfectly well what lay there—Upper Dam, with its sawmill and hotel, and the lakes above it.

"This is the nearest I ever been to Upper Dam," Gerrish said quietly. "I'd like to go there sometime, when it's convenient. 'Tain't much of a walk, they tell me—only about a quarter of a mile. But somehow when we're up this way, we always seem to be pushed."

"I've been to Upper Dam," I told him. "It isn't so much to see. What I'd like to see is the upper lakes." I was silent, thinking of their names. Mooselucmeguntic, Cupsuptic, Aziscoos. What would lakes with such lovely resounding names be like? There'd be something special and strange about them, I was sure. If only—I looked at Gerrish and he looked at me, and in that moment I knew I'd found a fellow renegade. I knew he wanted to go on a whirl around the lakes, too.

All we needed was to find a good excuse, and in this country a good excuse for taking a plain canoe trip takes some finding. We couldn't very well pose as timber cruisers or government surveyors. We were too well known. There was only one other alternative whereby we could go and still save our honor. We'd have to find some sports—city slickers or vacationists or dudes (take your choice)—who wanted to go and whom we could accompany in some plausible capacity such as hostess, guide, or long-suffering friends. It took us three years to do it.

My literary agent is a man named Willis Wing and he has a wife named Barbara. I suppose in most businesses it's all right if you don't like your associates, just as long as you are convinced of their honesty and competence. In the writing racket it is different, or so it seems to me. Writing is a very personal matter. When you sell a carload of grain or an electric refrigerator, nothing of yourself is involved. You make the deal, deliver the goods, collect the tariff, and kiss your client good-bye. When you sell a book or a story you are selling a part of your own identity. No matter how impersonal the subject matter may seem to the casual reader, it is colored by the writer's personal bias, animated by the Self of the writer. I never have and probably never will allow the members of my family or my best friends to read a manuscript of mine; I'd as soon undress on Boston Common. If the thing has merit enough so that some poor misguided editor will buy and print it, that's another matter. I enter the Public Domain, then—and, besides, there is something about printer's ink and the printed page that erects a screen between the reader and the writer, something mechanical and unimpassioned. But when a piece is in manuscript form, it is to me—and although I may be acting a little psychopathic about this I know other writers who feel the same way—as private as a love letter. That's why it is necessary for me at least to have an agent whom I not only trust in matters of money and ability, but whom I also like and upon whose sympathy I can depend. He has to read my manuscript. He has to write me letters saying, "Louise, that's a nice bit of work," or "Louise, have you gone nuts? That last story of yours is terrible." If I didn't like him as a person I couldn't stand the idea of having him view my exposed soul. If this be temperament—and in my book "temperament" is just a dressier word for a "rotten disposition"—make the most of it. And it's just so much meringue on the pie that I consider Willis Wing's wife to be one of my best friends. So——

The Wings would love to go on a canoe trip, it turned out. The night I got that letter, Gerrish and I exchanged furtive looks of congratulation over our baked beans and brown bread and started planning the expedition.

"There'll be the Wings and Ralph and I," I said. "Ralph?" He nodded resignedly, so I went on. "We ought to have two guides. You'll be one, of course, Gerrish, and maybe we can get hold of John Lavorgna." John Lavorgna is the first Maine guide I ever ran up against, years ago when my sister and I were white-collar girls vacationing in Maine on the hard-accumulated funds we'd scraped the bottom of the barrel all winter to amass; and he is still—when I've known a lot of guides and known them well—about the best. "Catherine will take care of the kids, of course. We'll get John to furnish the equipment. He's had a lot of experience in running trips. Everything is under control. We've got nothing to worry about."

Oh, how I had my neck out! The first thing that happened was that the Wing kids got the measles, so the trip had to be postponed a week. Then Ralph came down with an indisposition which has been referred to ever since as his "Mys-

terious Oriental Disease." He had one symptom: a temperature of 104.5 twenty-four hours a day for five days, unac-
companied by any ache or pain. So I arranged for an ambu-
lance to meet us at South Arm and had him carted off to the
hospital. Apparently that was all he needed, because when
he arrived there his temperature was normal, so I canceled
my next stop at Western Union, where I was going to send a
telegram to the Wings saying it was all off. Then, purely
out of unconstructive curiosity, I asked the doctor what had
ailed Ralph anyhow.

He said wisely, "A virus infection."

"Yeah," I said. "What does that mean?"

He laughed. "Nobody knows." That being the case we
changed the name to Mysterious Oriental Disease. It sounds
more interesting.

The morning when we finally, *mirabile dictu,* did get
started on the canoe trip was simply heavenly. Not a breath
of wind stirred and the hills about the lake stood toe to toe
with their reflections on the glassy surface. We rode down
to South Arm, where we were to meet John Lavorgna, on the
mail boat, congratulating each other on our great good luck
in drawing such a marvelous day out of the grab bag of the
weather. In a few minutes John drew up in a truck with three
canoes lashed on the top and the body filled with sleeping
bags, blankets, and food. We helped unload, slid the canoes
into the water, and drew lots as to who would team with
whom. John drew Barbara Wing, Willis and Ralph fell to
each other's lot, and Gerrish was stuck with me. This arrangement would last the whole three days of the trip, because it's a lot easier to continue with a bowman to whose
rhythm and eccentricities you have become accustomed than
it is to break in a new one every day. We shoved off just as a

cat's-paw darkened the milky blue of the water. It was the merest puff of air, gone almost before we saw its trace, truly like the swooping velvet caress of the kitten's paw for which it is named; but Ralph and John looked dubious and clucked their tongues. We were in for some tough paddling, they said, in what seemed to me to be a trouble-borrowing mood.

Before we really got the feel of the paddles we were plowing into two-foot swells. I don't know how the static mass of the tons of water could get to rolling so quickly, but it could. We worked, and I don't mean maybe. The thing about paddling a canoe is this: When you first start out after not having pushed one around for a while, you make a conscious effort with every stroke. You pick the blade up, thrust its head into the water, lean on it, swing it out and around, and start all over again. Your arms start aching and you feel the incipient blisters and you get a crick in your shoulders. You think, "Why was I ever fool enough to let myself in for this? We aren't even past Middle Dam yet, and we've got fifteen more miles to cover to-day. And fifteen, to-morrow. And the next day. And my arms are dropping off right this minute. I'll never be able to take it." Then after an interval in hell you discover that your aches and cricks have vanished and you are paddling automatically, the operation completely apart from your personal life. It's like breathing or the beat of the heart, which goes on no matter what you are thinking or doing. You're looking around at the scenery and exchanging remarks with your partner. It's then that a canoe trip starts to be fun. It entered that happy phase with me about the time we made the Narrows, with five miles behind us, and it was fun from then on.

The wind continued to blow. We stopped at Pine Island

for lunch, and some time while we were eating, a dense haze drifted in over the lakes. One minute we could see all over the world, and the next we couldn't see anything. It wasn't a true fog, which is dank and chilling. Inland fog doesn't associate with wind, anyhow. This was almost like smoke, dry and faintly luminous, lacking only the sweet, pungent smell of smoke. The wind had no power to dispel it, although it blew harder and harder, rolling the waves in from the northwest and hurling them to death at our feet on the sandy shore. The nearer ones were clear and green, with creaming tops and a hissing velocity about them. Those fifty feet offshore began to dim in outline, becoming motion without definition. Ten feet beyond that we could see only the gleaming crests, apparently materializing out of a limitless void. It was against nature, but it was lovely.

We'd planned to go on to Upper Dam before nightfall, but it seemed smarter to stay where we were until the wind went down and the haze thinned. In that murk we could lose touch with each other entirely, and if one of us capsized the others might paddle frantically in circles trying in vain to locate the cries for help. We didn't intend anything like that to happen, but it could. As John pointed out, you don't get drowned by staying on dry land. We decided to stay on dry land and amuse ourselves there for the rest of the day.

Connecting Pine Island with the mainland on the east is a narrow spit of white sand. This continues north on the mainland as a wide white beach. The Wings and Ralph and I walked over there to go swimming. The beach disappeared ahead of us into the haze and faded out behind us as we progressed. The waves came endlessly in from nowhere on our left, and all along the upper fringe of the sand, against the dark of the forest, were great pieces of dryki, looking like the

skeletons of prehistoric monsters. Dryki, in case you didn't
know, is long-dead wood—not logs, but whole trees, or complete gigantic root systems. They are the result of the raising
of the lake level by dams and the subsequent killing of the
trees that lie below the new water line. The bark has long
since fallen away and the wood has been scoured by sand and
wind and water and bleached by the sun out of all semblance
to the original tree. There is something tortured about these
strange, misshapen forms, something suggestive of hideous
death in proud agony. Lying there as they did, in a scene
divorced as it was from any context by the haze, they affected
us all, I am sure, oddly. We felt as though we were moving
through a landscape conceived and executed by a cosmic
Dali; as though we were wandering in a world between
worlds, where nothing we did or said could be held against
us, because we were nonexistent in a nonexistent place outside of time. I can remember it was almost with a feeling of
being rescued, from what un-nameable peril I cannot say,
that we heard John shout from over on the island that supper was ready. We came back to such homely and familiar
things as the smell of coffee, the sputter of steak in a pan,
and the sight of the two guides puttering around the fire as
domestically as two housewives in a country kitchen.

We thought that the wind would go down at sunset, but it
didn't. It blew all night long. We slept on the ground and
heard it rush over us in the treetops, roaring with a hushed
power. The waves rolled up on the beach, sighing and hissing and retreating reluctantly with a soughing drag. A little
after midnight a sudden, sharp shower rode up on the back
of the wind. Cool water was flung into our faces as they
lay exposed to the sky. We pulled the tarps over our heads
and lay quiet and warm, listening to the feet of the rain as

it trod briefly over us. Its footsteps faded into distance, treading with diminishing authority over the mountain toward the coast and the Atlantic and England. We slept. Dawn came, and the wind and the haze still held. It was phenomenal.

We decided after breakfast—the kind of breakfast that Maine guides consider obligatory: fruit, coffee, bacon, eggs, pancakes, fried potatoes, doughnuts, and last night's pie— that since we were supposed to be on a canoe trip, let's go on a canoe trip. The haze is a little thinner this morning, isn't it? Or isn't it? Anyhow, let's get going. Let's stay close together, holler like hell when in trouble, and take a chance. We can all swim.

So we set out. The haze actually was a little thinner until we got to Upper Dam. We could more or less see where we were going. The wind still blew, but our proficiency of the yesterday held. We could work into four-foot rollers with a feeling of exhilaration at the rise and drop, and at the sight of the crests boiling an inch below the gunwale. We'd found ourselves. We knew what we and our craft could do. We came with a sense of minor triumph into Upper Dam. Nobody was surprised to see us.

The grapevine had been at work. I don't understand its working yet, but that it does work is beyond argument. It isn't done with mirrors or smoke puffs, I know. My own theory is that its efficiency is based entirely upon the complete familiarity with the country of all its inhabitants. Any phenomenon outside the normal is observed and correctly interpreted, and when two observers trade notes all is laid bare. You might just as well have published your secret activities in the paper. We hadn't seen a soul the day before, but perhaps someone puttering past Pine Island in an outboard had smelled the smoke of our fire. They'd thought to themselves, "Now who in hell?"—and remembered that their cousin had seen John Lavorgna up on Parmachene the week before, and John had said he was going on a trip with the Riches. This then must be the Riches. So they'd told Mrs. Grant at Upper Dam that the Riches were on their way, and sure enough, the Riches showed up on schedule. Mrs. Grant greeted us cordially, we bought postcards while the canoes and duffle were being toted across the carry, and set off up Mooselucmeguntic.

Mooselucmeguntic is purely the sports' name for the lake above Upper Dam. To us it is always the Big Lake. It is a big lake, too, and they say it is a beautiful one. We wouldn't know. All day long we paddled in a haze that erased all shore lines, into a wind that showed no sign of letting up. The sun moved into the sky over our heads and shone with a bright diffuse light all about us. In spite of the wind it was hot. It was hot enough to burn off the haze, but it didn't. We met the big white boat that carries the mail from Oquossoc to Upper Dam. It was impossible to see her outline. She passed us, a flash of white and the sound of a motor droning and of voices speaking and answering each other. "—said it was trouble with the carburetor," said one; and a deep, throbbing voice answered, "Sooner think it was the gas line." Now and then small boats appeared out of nowhere, sharp figures silhouetted on the edge of the void. Once we saw, dark against the luminous curtain of the haze, a little boat in which stood two men struggling, while a third sat motionless in the stern and watched them. What were they fighting about? We didn't know. Why was the third man so unconcerned? They vanished as quickly as they had appeared, without a sound. It was as if we had ventured into some

Stygian half-world, where shades in ghostly barks continued old quarrels to which there would never be an end.

"Tell you one thing," said John, twenty feet off Gerrish's and my port bow. "Any sport of mine stands up in a boat and starts fighting, I'd hit him over the head with a oar. Goddam fools. Good way to get drowned."

And still the wind blew. I never heard of such a wind. I said to Gerrish once, when the blisters on my hands were getting a little too sore for complete comfort, "When we get around the next corner, it ought to be behind us. Then we can coast a minute."

He corrected me kindly, in the manner of one speaking to a not-quite-bright child: "You mean when we round the point into the lee, she'll be astern and we can run before her." That was probably what I meant, but it never worked out that way. Every time we changed course, the wind shifted, too. This sounds improbable, but I have five witnesses that it was true. Never once on the whole circuit of the trip did we have anything but a full head wind. At first we thought nothing of it; then we became annoyed; and finally we grew rather proud of a wind so malicious. It was our personal wind, damn it!

I'd never be able again to find the place where we had lunch. I don't know how John did it. At noon he pointed into the fog and said, "Over there is where we stop to eat." We obediently headed Over There and in a minute saw the white glimmer of a grove of birches. Out of nowhere a clean, stony little beach resolved itself. We hauled the canoes up and took a thread of path through tall grasses and raspberry canes into a clearing under the birches. It was a lovely spot, all the lovelier for having apparently been materialized out of the impalpable substance of the fog by the magical point-

ing of John's silver-dripping paddle. We built a fire and ate
corn chowder and chocolate cake and were just about to
re-embark when Ralph discovered that the tall growth of
raspberry and the bristling thicket of fir and spruce hid the
remains of what once had been an elaborate camp. Gerrish
and I looked at each other and groaned. Gerrish put down
the packsack he had started to carry down to the canoes, lay
down under a tree, and tipped his hat over his face. I salvaged a cup and started picking raspberries. We both knew
from long experience that we were there for some time to
come.

Long years of living in the woods where the general rule
is to fix up what you have or go without had developed in
Ralph an absolute mania for junk. I think he saw every bit
of territory he covered, not in the light of scenic or geo-
graphic interest, but in that of possible salvage. He'd say,
when rigging up an old car motor into a winch, "What I
need is a three foot piece of one-inch angle iron." Then
he'd squat on his heels and stare into space with the unseeing
stare you sometimes see in a cat. At the end of a minute he'd
announce, "and I know where there is one." It might be
three miles away at Sunday Pond, or at South Arm, or over
at Black Cat where a sawmill burned down fifteen years ago;
but it would be there. I never used to be able to understand
how he could be so sure, but I finally got that way myself.
Once you get the junkman's eye, the mental cataloguing of
junk becomes subconscious. I remember Ralph's saying to
me once, "I wish I had a piece of strap iron," and hearing
my own voice answer without conscious volition, "There's
one over by B Pond, about six feet long with half-inch holes
bored at foot intervals." It wasn't until I'd said it that I
realized that it was true. I did know where there was one—in

the yard of Thurston's old Number Three camp, long since deserted and fallen down, lying on a rock near the spring. I honestly don't remember ever especially noticing that piece of iron; but when we walked over the ridge to look, sure enough, it was there.

As it turned out, this new junk mine wasn't very profitable. Most of the metal—and there was quite a lot—was galvanized stock, and therefore inferior. I found a good piece of iron rod just the wrong length to be conveyed comfortably in a canoe. It wouldn't lie quite flat on the bottom, so that every time you got in or out the darn thing tripped you. In addition, it periodically stabbed me, sitting in the bow seat, just over the kidney. But we took it all the rest of the way around the lakes and safely home. It's in the woodshed right now, awaiting its final fate, not yet determined. It'll probably end up as strengthener in a cement fill.

That afternoon we spent looking for corpses. John planted this enchanting notion in our minds just after we left the lunch ground and were again headed into the teeth of the wind. We now had to cross the widest part of the lake and would be out of sight of land for an hour or so. John said cheerfully, "The way she's rolling up, those Frenchmen ought to be coming to the top. Water's warm now. They ought to be ready to float." About two months before, two men had been drowned on this stretch of the lake under rather mysterious circumstances. Their bodies had never been recovered, a thing in itself peculiar. Although people who drown in the fall are often not recovered until spring, the bodies always do rise to the surface when the warming of the water hastens disintegration with its accompanying release of buoyant body gases. These Frenchmen should have come up as soon as the spring chill was out of the water; but they hadn't, and never have to this very day. I don't know whether John believed his own story or whether he thought we might be bored with nothing to look at but the haze and the rolling water. At any rate, he had us seeing in every floating branch or drifting log, a dead man about to climb aboard. It lent a certain spice to the crossing, but I'm glad we didn't find them.

One of the most delightful things about that afternoon's paddle through the windy, sun-shot haze was the social aspect of it. It had some of the characteristics of a big reception where you mill about with a cocktail glass in your hand, performing conversational gymnastics. You talk first with one person about the international situation, then to another about the artistic merits of the newest play, and then to a gentleman from Illinois about the trials of strip mining. We didn't have cocktail glasses in our hands—only paddles; we weren't milling aimlessly in our best clothes but working like hell against a head wind in blue denims and checked shirts; our conversational gambits were far from orthodox; but the effect was the same. Due to the vagaries of the wind and of our own canoemanship, the nature of the group was fluid. I was alone with Gerrish, for example, when he said, "Why don't you take that sweater off?"

"With the wind blowing like this? Wild horses couldn't get this sweater off me!"

"You know"—Gerrish was thoughtful—"whenever I hear that expression, I get to wondering. I wonder just how a wild horse would go about getting that sweater off you. 'Twould be kind of interesting to see."

I giggled and we went on from there analyzing stock phrases until John and Barbara plowed within hearing. They were, for some unimaginable reason, discussing the best way to catch flies with your hands. John was expounding the theory that flies take off backward, so the thing to do is to swoop down on them from the rear. This led to a discussion of the killing of mosquitoes between clapped hands and agreement on the fact that if your hands are dripping wet, you can almost always get them. Gerrish's idea was that their wings stick in the water, while I had a very fancy notion that the water makes a cushion for the air, so there's no draft to blow the little stinkers to safety. We continued the argument on a crescendo until they were out of earshot and we overtook Willis and Ralph. They were being very serious on the subject of getting into a rut. I don't know about whom they were talking, but I took advantage of the situation to remark that a rut was what other people got into; when it was yourself, you were living in tune with life's rhythm. They both looked disgusted, so I went on to add that I didn't see anything the matter with a rut, anyhow. There are ruts and ruts. If you pick yourself a nice broad one, you can have a good time and a certain amount of variety without sacrificing to adventure the elements of peace and security. Willis was just saying, "Yes, but when things get too easy and secure, it's time to move on," when they blew out of shouting distance. Gerrish told me that we were shipping a little water and I'd better move the oatmeal to a dry spot. I did so, getting jabbed in the back with the salvaged iron rod in the process, and he said, "Reminds me when I was a kid we used to have Quaker Oats. There was a Quaker on the box holding a box of Quaker Oats in his hand, and on that box was another Quaker, holding a box, and on that box—used to drive me crazy wondering where it stopped. I couldn't puzzle out where it would ever stop,

supposing you had eyes good enough to see them, no matter how small they got."

This fascinated me, because I had received my first inti-
mation of infinity from a box of Quaker Oats, too. So we
talked that over. That's the kind of conversational afternoon
that we spent, and I, for one, enjoyed it.

After the first twenty-four hours of a canoe trip, a peculiar
unity is developed. This is partly, of course, because the
members of the group are being subjected to a day-and-night
exposure to each other under conditions that allow for little
privacy. But it is also due, I think, to the nature of the trip.
If you are traveling by car or train, you are dependent to
some extent on the outside world. Someone else is responsible for your locomotion. You buy food in restaurants and
sleep in hotel beds. On a canoe trip you take your world
with you. Everything that you need to be self-sufficient is in
the pile of duffle amidships—blankets, food, dishes, dry
socks, everything. You feel, "Here we are together, working
on a common enterprise, cut off from the rest of the world.
So to hell with everyone else. We don't owe them anything—
only each other." On most trips you do encounter other
people, but you feel toward them a curious detachment that
is the antithesis of the solidarity and rapport you feel in your
own group. You have your own catchwords, the significance
of which no one else understands. You build up, even in one
day, a whole body of lore and habit and attitude that ex-
cludes the rest of the world. It's a very hard thing to explain,
but it's one of the things that gives such a trip a very special
quality and flavor. It's a thing everyone should experience
at least once in his life—this feeling of complete identity
with a group, of selfless devotion, both physical and men-

tal, to the good of that group. We'd developed it well by the time we came to Cupsuptic.

I imagine that Cupsuptic is a very beautiful lake. What little we saw of it was lovely. After we'd crossed what we called Dead Frenchman Bay we saw something huge and white and shining in the haze. It was there for a moment and then gone, but John said it was the Mountain View House and we were about to enter the narrows between Mooselucmeguntic and Cupsuptic. Here our course turned an abrupt right angle and we again foolishly anticipated a wind that would be at least quartering. Experience should have taught us better. We rounded Blueberry Island, the wind immediately shifted into the north, and again we were plowing straight into it. We hugged the shore, so we did get an idea of the character of the lake. The Rangeleys down our own way have black growth clear to the water's edge, with an occasional small sandy beach. Cupsuptic is all ledges, and if there is anything I love, it's ledges of living rock, crowned with tall firs and dropping sheer into deep water. We saw just enough of Cupsuptic's shore line to whet my appetite to go back and see more some day.

We had to stop at Pleasant Island, where there is a sporting camp, to arrange for a truck to take us over the road to the headwaters of the Magalloway the next morning, and while we were waiting for John to finish the transaction, Barbara Wing, who weighs about one hundred and twenty pounds, ate an ice-cream cone and four nut-marshmallow-chocolate bars. That's the chief thing I remember about that place. Then we went across to a little island, pitched camp, had supper, and went to bed. The next morning we were transported across to Aziscoos Dam, where the Magalloway starts.

The Magalloway River is never referred to in our family as anything but the "Noble Magalloway." This is because we once read a book, vintage of about 1880, called *Gaunt Gurley, or The Trapper of Umbagog*. True to the literary standards of the day, the author employed to express his stilted sentiments a very lofty and flowery style, and his characters were always racing up and down the calm bosom of the "noble" Magalloway. The Magalloway must have changed since then. We didn't think it so very noble. It's a fair-sized stream meandering down a valley between low mud banks. The wind had gone down at last, just when we could have done with a little of it, and the sun glared through the still-existent haze with all the searing intensity of a burning glass. We felt as though we were confined in a Turkish bath under violet ray. I lost one of my shoes overboard and never saw it again.

But after ten years of daily conversation with Joe Mooney, I did at last get to see him. I walked into the office at the Brown Farm and said, "Hello, Joe."

He turned around and said, "Why, hello, Louise."

I said, disappointed that my surprise hadn't worked, "Oh, you knew we were coming"; and he said, "No, I recognized your voice." Joe can recognize anybody's voice, even if he hasn't heard it for ten years, and then only over the telephone. He's remarkable. People try to fool him, but they never can. "What in hell are you doing over here?" he wanted to know now.

Ralph explained, "We're on a canoe trip," and Joe asked, "You gone crazy?"

Ralph said, "No, we've got some people from New York staying with us," and Joe said, "Oh," with sympathy and understanding. And that was that. We struck out again down the Noble Magalloway toward Umbagog.

Mr. Leman's flag was out on Pine Point, so we stopped in there to call on him. This, of course, was before we had bought the place ourselves. He invited us to spend the night, and although we could have reached home before dark, we stayed. That was the first night I ever slept at Pine Point. I was going to say "under the roof of Pine Point," but that would not be accurate. John, Gerrish, and Ralph accepted the offer of good beds, but Willis and Barbara and I didn't. We were roughing it, so we felt an obscure obligation to rough it to the bitter end. We spread our blankets on the dock and slept there, fools that we were. Or were we? The moon rode high and full and gold through the blur of the haze, and the waves slapped gently at our heads and feet. The boats knocked softly at their moorings and out on the lake a loon called and called and then laughed its hysterical laughter. It was lovely and otherworldly; but the planks got awfully hard before morning.

The next morning it rained. We didn't care. We were almost home anyhow and we'd had a wonderful time. Mr. Leman took us to Sunday Cove in the *Puss,* towing the canoes behind, and we sat on the gunwales with the rain streaming down our faces and soaking our shirts, while we went over and over the events of the whirl around the lakes. "Remember that boat on the Big Lake?" we asked each other, as reminiscently as though the boat had been a feature of the Battle of the Wilderness and we were hoary-headed veterans in convention. "Remember the *wind*!" The aura of the canoe trip still surrounded us thickly.

But not for long. Catherine had left the children in charge of her sister while she drove down to the Cove to get us, and they greeted us enthusiastically as we came into the yard. They'd been out playing in the rain, and they weren't wearing a stitch of clothes among them, unless you count the turbans they were modeling on each other's heads. These were made of mud and cement, which they had found in the woodshed, and were about the size of basketballs. "Oh, my God!" I groaned, and wondered how much hot water there was in the stove tank. Very definitely, we were home again.

CHAPTER V

Pine Point

Have you ever seen a place—a house, a meadow lying lazy in the sun, a walled garden, a reedy bend of river—and felt, finally and beyond argument, "That's mine"? It might have been only a glimpse from a train window of a place you knew you'd never again lay eyes on, but something quick and compelling sprang up in the heart at the sight, and when you were past you'd left a part of yourself there, forever. The real owner, in terms of money and deeds and taxes, could continue to think that it was his; you were doing him no harm nor encroaching upon his rights. Nevertheless, it was yours. You held a spiritual lease on it that nothing could nullify, and no court of law in the land could take it out of your secret life. It was yours.

That's the way I felt about Pine Point the first time I ever saw it, and that's the way I still feel. I was taught in school—more years ago than I like to remember—that we must be careful about the use of the word "love" since it is possible to love only animate objects who can return the compliment. All right, Miss Bennett and Miss Burnell and Miss Davis, and all the other Misses who contributed to what I fondly call my education. In your bright lexicon one can't love a house and a view and five hundred acres of woodland, bound by seven miles of shoreline. I still love Pine Point.

Pine Point, reduced to simple words, is a peninsula in Umbagog, the next lake down the chain from Forest Lodge. There are millions of trees growing on it, and on the westernmost tip, a group of buildings. The only way you can get to it with any degree of comfort is by boat, for while it is not entirely surrounded by water, it might just as well be. There is no road anywhere near it, and although, if you must, you can get out in an emergency, it would have to be a pretty dire emergency to sell anyone the idea of walking miles through the sort of wilderness that lies back of Pine Point. The place used to be owned by a Mr. Leman and now it is owned by a Mrs. Rich. That's Pine Point.

Oh, why do I try to be coldblooded about it when I think of it always in terms of poetry? I can't write poetry myself—or only very poor verse for my own benefit—but other people can and do, and many of them say the things I feel about Pine Point in words I couldn't muster. Malcolm Cowley said them in *The Long Voyage:*

> Not that the pines are darker, there,
> nor midway dogwood brighter there,
> nor swifts more swift in summer air:
>   it was my own country,
>
> having its thunderclap of spring,
> its long midsummer ripening,
> its corn hoar-stiff at harvesting,
>   almost like any country,
>
> yet being mine, its face, its speech,
> its hills bent low within my reach,
> its river birch and upland beech
>   were mine, of my own country.*

* From *The Dry Season* by Malcolm Cowley. Copyright in 1941 by Malcolm Cowley. Published by New Directions.

That's how I feel about Pine Point.

It's a long, low, wooded, rocky point, jutting out into the lake, and every time, after an absence, I see its outline against the sky, my heart almost bursts. It looks so—I don't know. Solitary, proud, complete. I lean over the side of the boat and strain my eyes for the first glimpse of the house, hidden in pines and birches at the land's end. First you can see the guides' house and the clothesyard. Then you can see the powerhouse, which shelters the Kohler for lights and the pump for water. Then you round the rock and the flagpole, and through the trees you can see the chimney and roof of the main house. There is something about that roof and chimney—something about its low, slow sweep and solid lines—that is like a benediction.

Yes, I know I'm being overemotional about a parcel of property—but when did it ever hurt a heart to love a piece of the earth, a rock-solid foundation, a rooftree and sheltering walls? I have an artist friend named Vee Akers—and a very good artist he is—who speaks sometimes of what he calls the "Presence" of a place. Some places, like some people, lack presence. Pine Point does not. It is filled with a great, brooding peace. No one who has ever been there has failed to feel it. The sun lies softly upon it, and the air is always full of the two loveliest sounds on earth, the wash of water upon stone, the sound of wind in trees. No breeze that stirs evades it, situated as it is with open lake on all sides, and the air moves sweetly all day long through the open windows of the house.

Let me tell you about the house. It is built like a fort. After being at Pine Point, when I enter any other house I feel as if it were going to collapse like a house of cards, about my ears. The rafters are all eight-by-eight hewn pine, where other houses have four-by-four. Wherever another house has an inch board for a shelf, in Pine Point you find a two-inch plank. The living-room is two stories high, with a fieldstone fireplace that will take four-foot logs. The shingles on the outer walls are two feet long, with two-inch butts. They're a lot of shingle. Every room has a stove, set on a stone hearth that springs from the earth, so that they are solid and firm and fireproof. The windows swing outward on hinges, and I've never known one to stick. The place is well built. I admire good carpentry, myself. The porches are twelve feet wide, screened with fine copper screen. The rain never beats in there, because of the wide overhang of eave; so in the summer the children sleep on the porches, partly because I think it's good for them, and partly because they like it. I remember when I was a child I liked to lie in bed, on a broad, bright night, and look out of the window. So do my children. They lie there in a row, with their visiting friends, and stare out at the high, white moon. Many and many a night have I gone out, just before my bedtime, to be sure all was well, and found ten young faces, tranced and still above the red of the blankets and the turned-over white of the sheets, watching that far dead world climb the heavens behind the pines. They won't forget. Decades from now, in places removed in time and space, they will remember those nights, and the peace, and the beauty. They will remember and be reassured and strong.

Mr. Leman built the place—which is really a glorified camp—according to his own notions. He could afford to do so, and since he felt the same way about the Point as I do, apparently, he really put his heart into it. He liked things massive and lasting, and he certainly got them.

Let me tell you about Mr. Leman. When I first met him

he was a man of over seventy, and one of the most charming persons I have ever met. He had beautiful manners, which aren't the basis of charm, of course, but they certainly help. Under them he had a lively intelligence, a keen and subtle wit, sophistication, and a friendly soul. Starting from scratch, as a boy, he had amassed a lot of money, so I guess he was also very shrewd. Having lived in his house for two years, I now know he was also in some ways very young and naïve.

Have you ever taken over anyone else's house, lock, stock, and barrel? It's a very revealing procedure. When he sold the place to Ralph and me, everything was included, except his personal belongings, such as clothes and the shaving kit on the bathroom shelf—everything from the andirons in the fireplace, to the teakettle on the kitchen range, to the coonskin cap done up in mothballs in the attic. There were linen and silver and blankets and dishes; there were a zither and books and the mounted bear and deer heads and birds in the living-room; there were boats and duck-calls and silk tents. There was everything.

And that's how I know so much about Mr. Leman that I'd feel embarrassed to meet him again. I couldn't think of him in any less formal way than Mister—it would smack of impertinence in view of his age and lovely formal manner— but the fact remains that I know so much about him that I feel like a very unpleasant snoop. I feel that I have violated his privacy—I, who cherish personal privacy of mind more than anything—to a simply appalling degree. I'm certain he would be outraged if he realized how much I know about him.

I know, for example, that he is childish, as am I, about some things. Up in the attic there is the most marvelous collection of wooden boxes with tight-fitting covers that I ever saw. I dearly love a wooden box with a good cover, so I go up there and gloat over them like a miser. I wouldn't use one for the world, and I know Mr. Leman felt the same way. The whole house is full of things put away in battered suit boxes, things which would be much better stored in wood. The sensible thing to do would be to take a day off and repack them in the boxes up in the attic; but I can't do it. Neither, apparently, could Mr. Leman. He, as I, was silly about a wooden box.

I know that under his shrewdness lay a certain amount of gullibility and trustfulness. When I asked him where he had bought his dinner dishes—a full set for twenty-four, and very handsome, indeed—he told me, and added, "But if you're thinking of replacing breakage, come with me." We made sure his cook wasn't watching—this was before the Riches took over—and sneaked up the ladder that leads from the living-room into the attic. There in a dark closet under the eaves; pushed back behind the spare mattresses, was a whole boxful of cups and cream pitchers which, everyone knows, have a high mortality rate. "Don't tell your help about these," Mr. Leman advised me in a conspiratorial undertone: "If they know you have extras, they'll be careless."

I was speechless with admiration for his acumen.

But last spring I took my Catherine up to look the situation over, knowing I could trust her not to take advantage. The box was there, all right, but half the pitchers were cracked and half the cups had no handles. Mr. Leman had been away a lot, when he lived here. It was pretty trusting of him to believe that his help didn't investigate during his absence what lay in every corner of the attic. It was pretty simple of him to think that the cook would confess to a broken cup when all she had to do was wait her chance to exchange it for a whole one.

When Mr. Leman built this house, he inaugurated a few features of his own design, some of which he pointed to with pride when he showed us over the place. One is the ledge over the kitchen sink, which, instead of being flat, slopes at an angle of forty-five degrees. I thought at the time he was mentioning it to me that his cook gave him a look of combined hate and frustration, but that seemed improbable. It was undoubtedly, I decided, a trick of the light.

But a few months later Catherine had to go Outside for a day or two, and I did my own cooking. I'm here to say that no trick of the light was responsible for that cook's look. Of all the fiendish arrangements, that is the worst. There it is in front of you, as you wash the dishes, a lovely ledge, eight inches wide, smooth and empty, ideal for up-ending Mason jars to drain, or for storing the soap-powder box or the can you keep used corks in. Or it would be if it didn't slope. It drives you mad. I know as well as Mr. Leman did, that a flat, pine ledge over the sink means eventually a messy hoo-rah's nest over the sink; but I still think even that would be preferable to violent insanity in whoever does the dishes. Mr. Leman, I'm afraid, had a sadistic streak.

There is a lot to be said for taking over someone else's house, completely furnished. For one thing, you can take a detached attitude toward it. When someone comes in and exclaims, "Oh, what a lovely room!"—and they do, about the living-room—you can agree without giggling coyly and saying, "Well, *we* like it." Sure, it's a lovely room and since I wasn't responsible for it, I can admit that I think so, too. I like the wide windows and deep windowseats. I think the long, horizontal poles suspended from the roof beams by

ropes and used to hang colorful rugs and blankets on—or
wet socks and coats to be dried, or the baby's diapers—are a
fine idea. They bring the high ceiling down without inter-
fering with air circulation, they are convenient, and they
add color and atmosphere. I think the bulletin board on the
wall by the door is a good notion, too. It saves a lot of talking.

Let me tell you about that bulletin board. It's about a
yard square, and on the shelf beneath is a box of thumb-
tacks. In every guestroom, posted on the mirror, is a little
notice: *Please read the bulletin board in the living-room before you go further.* Some of Mr. Leman's pronouncements
I've had to abandon. He, for example, had set meal hours,
outlined on the board, and the guest was supposed to be
present with his face washed, on time. We have our meals
when we get around to it. So my ruling is that we'll let you
know when we eat, you can have breakfast any time you
want, but after 9 A.M. you can't have eggs or anything else
cooked to order. You'll eat fruit, toast, and coffee; and if you
don't like it, get yourself out of bed earlier to-morrow. But
I have kept his attitude about some other things. One is that
we cleaned your room and made up your bed before you got
here. From now on, if you want your bed made, make it
yourself. Another is that if you want a towel to take down
onto a dock or into a boat, ask Catherine for an old one.
Don't take my best blue bathtowels, which you'll find in
your room. I don't want them ruined. Another is that you
are welcome to read any book, or use any equipment, but
God help you if you don't put it back where you found it.
And please, when you're through with a canoe, leave it
bottomside up on the float, with the paddles underneath.
And please clean guns only in the guides' house, so if anyone

gets shot, it'll be you. And please don't go around spotting trees. People get lost following random spots. We have the trails all marked out. There are some more rulings, but this gives you the general idea; and can't you see that it prevents my sounding like an old harpy every time a guest does something wrong?

Another thing I like in the living-room are the two tables, one on either side of the fireplace. They are about ten feet long, three feet wide, and so heavy that it takes two people to move one. But that's not the remarkable thing about them. They are made of birch, but have the loveliest dark and glowing sheen I ever saw on wood. I thought they were stained, but they aren't. They were burned with a sulphuric acid wash, a coat at a time, until the right tone was attained—something between ebony and mahogany, with an underfire. This is a dangerous procedure, and should not be attempted by an amateur. They are lovely, and the way you keep them lovely is to rub them with bacon grease or any other kitchen grease, every once in a while. You do this with your bare hand, as the heat of the palm is just enough to melt the grease properly. This makes a fine rainy day occupation, when everyone is in the living-room, talking. You sit there and talk, too, but at the same time you are accomplishing something. You rub and rub by the hour, and decide that the public school system needs overhauling, and the new length of skirt is unbecoming to anyone except Marlene Dietrich and that someone should write a book about the relationship of specific mental attitudes to specific diseases. Then the sun comes out, or everyone says to hell with the rain, let's go swimming; so you take a paper towel, rub off the surplus grease, and there you are.

When we move annually from Forest Lodge to Pine

Point, we actually move only three miles as the crow flies—seven miles by jalopy and boat to us non-crows; but it's moving from one life to another. We move from a life of kerosene lamps, of water in pails for drinking and in galvanized tubs on the kitchen floor for bathing, of discreet little outhouses concealed behind fir thickets, to a life of electric lights, running hot and cold water, and a bathroom equipped with shower bath in addition to the usual features. This sounds sybaritic, but it's not quite what it sounds. We are not on a public power line, but generate our own light from a Kohler system, or private farm-type lighting plant. Most of the time that's wonderful, but once in a while it runs amok, and then we are without light or water for the period it takes to repair the damage. Lack of civilization isn't half so hard to cope with as a civilization which has broken down, leaving you with nothing to take its place. That's bad!

Even the nature of the country changes in that three miles. At Forest Lodge we are really in the woods, with the Rapid River boiling by the door and the view limited to the short vistas up- and down-river. At Pine Point we are on the lake, and we can see clear over into New Hampshire, where the deep clefts of the valleys of the Androscoggin and the Magalloway lead the eye west and north into the ramparts of the climbing hills. We can see, ten miles south of us, the rooftops of Upton over a ridge, and beyond them, fifty miles away, Mount Washington, alone and lofty and lovely.

Umbagog is, I think, the most beautiful lake I have ever seen. The mountains do not wall it in closely, as do the mountains surrounding the Richardson lakes, next above us in the chain. They stand back a little, rising in broad benches up and away. The shore line is irregular, so that every hundred feet of progress by canoe or boat down its length opens new and unsuspected vistas or reveals surprising, lovely little compositions of wood and rock and water. I think, in the hundreds of hours I have spent on and around the lake, I have never seen it look twice alike. The light changes; the visibility ranges from a smoky haze to a crystal clarity like the light of heaven; the surface lies mirrorlike and pearly or rolls against the shore in thundering ice-green, white-capped breakers. Umbagog is various and beautiful and strange.

And, as is often true of the beautiful and strange, Umbagog is a bitch—a dangerous, treacherous bitch. I'm not using that unpleasant word lightly, nor on my own responsibility. Ask anyone around here about Umbagog—ask Larry Parsons, or old Ben Bennett who has lived all his life on her shores, or Cliff Wiggin, who sometimes calls himself Cliff Wallace for variety's sake—and they'll all tell you the same thing in the same words. We all—we who live here and know —are afraid of Umbagog. We're never quite comfortable in our minds—and this is a dreadful thing to feel and say—until each year someone has been drowned there. I am not particularly brave but, on the other hand, I am not, I think, a complete physical coward; and one of the things I'm fairly indifferent to is water. I can swim not stylishly, but strongly. I'd rather go into the water on purpose than be pitched, wearing my best clothes, out of a boat. However, if all comes to all, as my friend Barbara Wing says, I could probably get ashore under my own power from anywhere on the lake. But —I am afraid of Umbagog.

It's hard to explain why. I guess it involves a personification of the lake. None of us can ever think of it as a body of water, governed by laws of physics and chemistry and meteorology and what-have-you. Umbagog is a power, sentient and demanding. She has to have her yearly blood offering. If it's not anybody else, it'll be you or your children, or someone near and dear to you. Call this superstition or paganism or what you will—it's true. I can't remember a year of my living here when someone was not drowned in Umbagog. The first year it was the caretaker of the Chandler camp. The next year it was five men from Berlin—found eventually washed up on the shores of Piñe Point, between the pump house and the clothesyard. Next year it was a bride and groom of twenty-four hours, on a hunting-trip honeymoon. Then there were the three hunters from Bethel. This year there was the man who fell off a dredger. Every year it's someone. You can say what you will, no other lake in the State has so bad a record. There's something about Umbagog——

One of the reasons, if we want to abandon folklore and get down to sense, is that the lake is very shallow and exposed to the winds that are drawn down the valleys about it, as air is drawn into a flue. This makes it susceptible to sudden squalls. The shallow water gets to rolling quickly, and unless you have been watching, you find yourself caught in what looks like a typhoon. I remember once Ralph and I were coming up from Upton in the *Puss*. Down below Jessie Potter's we met the New Hampshire game warden puttering along in an outboard. It was so dead calm that the smoke from his exhaust didn't dissipate at all, but lay inert on the black, slick surface of the lake, a static trail that we could follow up through the narrows without the usual bother and fuss of my having to stand up on the bow and look for the rather insignificant buoys that mark a very narrow channel between two reefs. I think I never saw the world so hushed nor water so glassy.

So we were paying no heed. Ralph sat on the pilot's stool, his feet tied in knots about the legs, and I leaned against the cabin door, watching the reflected autumn trees slide by. We were both smoking and were talking, I remember, about labor unions. I thought they had once been more than useful and he thought they'd always been a pain in the neck. We had just reached a tentative armistice when green water started coming in over the bow.

Now the *Puss* is a good boat. When water comes in over the bow, there is a sea running. We snapped to. Ralph said, "Hey! Start pumping!" just as I said, "Hey, Bud! You're way off the course!" We looked ahead and there was nothing but a smother of six-foot combers, piling tier on tier out of a black and murky curtain of low cloud. The wind smote us from the west with a devastating strength. We could see, hear, and feel nothing but wet and cold and that infernal pitching. I pumped for gosh-sake and Ralph hauled on the wheel. We had no idea where we were or where we were going. We hoped to God we were still fairly near the middle of the lake, and we thought maybe we were, since five minutes before all had been as sweet as pie and as calm as blancmange.

And five minutes later we returned to that happy, if stupid, condition. But those elapsed ten minutes could have drowned us, just as they had drowned twenty persons to my personal knowledge and twenty more that I know about. Oh, make no mistake. Umbagog is a bitch.

And that is why we have a fussy, fiddling, old-maid rule for our children, our help, our guests, and ourselves: You may not take out a boat, canoe, or any floating object unless you will promise faithfully and upon your honor to go ashore on the nearest shore the minute she starts to roll. Stay there. Only when it calms down can you come home, even if you have to stay two days. You may be cold and hungry and disgusted, but at least you aren't lying on the floor of Umbagog, nibbled at by fish, to arise eventually, bloated and ugly, to be picked at by the scavenging gulls. I'm painting an unpleasant picture, and if you'll forgive me, I'm doing it deliberately. I've seen some of Umbagog's victims. I don't care awfully much about having my own people join that unhappy throng.

Even our social life changes when we move to Pine Point. We see an altogether different group of people—people we never knew, with the exception of Cliff, and he has always been a telephone, rather than a face-to-face, acquaintance. While at Forest Lodge, we see the Millers and the Parsons and the various summer guests at the hotel. And that is that. Down on Umbagog people are very social. The first day I was ever there, we had callers. I'd forgotten that people made calls on new arrivals in a community, having lived for ten years in a static society where there were no newcomers. I was dressed snappily in a torn shirt, wet, rolled-up dungarees—I'd fallen into the lake during landing operations and had had no time to change—dirty sneakers and no socks, and I was hanging out the baby's diapers. It was three o'clock in the afternoon—of course, a decent calling hour—but somehow things had piled up on us that day, what with this and that. I looked up to see approaching along the boathouse path what looked to be a crowd of people. I was embarrassed.

I needn't have been. They were Phil and Nancy Hesseltine from across the lake on the New Hampshire side, with their son Stark and four house guests.

There are a lot of things I can say about the Hesseltines, but I'll start by saying that Nancy, besides being the very prettiest woman I ever saw as well as the nicest, is socially completely dependable. This is a rare attribute and one which I hope to inculcate in my own daughter. No matter what awful silence falls, what faux pas has been made, what heterogeneous group you may have inadvertently collected, you can count on Nancy to say and do the right thing. Ralph always insisted that this was a result of breeding, that Nancy is a *lady* in the good old solid sense of the word—the best sense. I differ. Breeding certainly has something to do with it, but it seems to me that social adequacy is based on more than surface polish. It's based, I think, on a kind heart, a selfless nature. All the adjectives I can think of to apply to Nancy have fallen into disrepute. She is sweet and kind and good, and doesn't that make her sound stupid! She's not stupid. She makes all the clever and self-sufficient and successful women of my acquaintance, all the bright, amusing career girls, ring as false as brass in comparison. I love Nancy, starting with the day when she didn't even notice that I was dirty and hot and disorganized, when I should at least have had my face washed and my hair combed.

I love Phil, too, and Ralph simply adored him. Phil not only felt as bitter about certain aspects of modern civilization as Ralph did, but he expressed his feelings in terms as caustic as Ralph's own. That takes some doing, since Ralph was never one to pull his verbal punches. One of the subjects they periodically raved about—and periodically means daily or every time they got together—was the Problem of the Flat-bottomed Frenchman. They'd both been victimized.

A flat-bottomed Frenchman, in case you didn't know, is a French Canadian who uses a flat-bottomed boat. The adjective has nothing to do with physiology, merely with nautical equipment. No one in his right mind in this country would be caught dead in a flat-bottom boat. We favor the Rangeley type, with a round bottom, or a canoe. All Frenchmen are not flat bottomed, any more than all Yankees are thieving horse traders; but a certain small group infests the lake in their unmentionable craft, which they store at Errol Dam. Using that as a base of operations, they wander up the Androscoggin to Umbagog, seeking what they may devour—or, more literally, steal. So far, all we've lost is an electric pump, a one-man crosscut saw, three boat cushions, an oil drum, and a pair of oars. Even I was irritated about the oars, as they were mine. I'd spent a lot of time on them, sanding them down after each of three coats of varnish, till they looked and felt like light molasses velvet. If ever I catch up with the son-of-a-seacook who took my oars—but I see I'm relapsing into the Phil-Ralph attitude and vocabulary.

You should hear Phil rant. After all, he's lost practically everything except his eyeteeth and the kitchen sink. They stole Stark's birthday-gift kyak, before the paint was even scratched on it. They stole the rope out of Phil's flagpole—and you have to have a flagpole on Umbagog, as the custom of the country dictates that when you are home and in a mood for visitors, you fly a flag. No flag, no one will call on you. They stole—and this must have been quite an engineering feat, when you consider that a flat-bottomed boat is small and not too seaworthy—Phil's grindstone, so that now, when he wants to put an edge on an ax, he has to paddle over to Pine Point and use ours. They broke into his camp and took his dishes and blankets. They took his oars out of his boat while he was on the innocent mission of collecting his mail in Errol. Retribution caught up with that particular malefactor, though. Proceeding up the Androscoggin on his way home, in what vile temper I need not outline, Phil overtook the miscreant rowing busily north. He throttled down his outboard and came alongside.

"Those are my oars," he announced coldly.

"Who said so?"

"I say so. They've got my name on them. Hand them over."

At this point in the account I asked timidly, "And did he?"

"No," said Phil with awful restraint. "But I got them." I didn't ask for details. Phil stands well over six feet and, while he is usually under control, I could see easily what he meant.

"But how'm I going to get home?" asked our flat-bottomed friend.

"That's your problem," Phil announced, and oars aboard, stepped up his motor. "Last I saw of the so-and-so," he concludes with satisfaction, "he was clawing his way along that channel boom toward Errol. Hope he had a nice trip. He only had four miles to go, the bastard!"

I'm indebted to Phil for a report of what I still consider the Meanest Trick of the Century, perpetrated by an F.-B. Frenchman. Phil, one fine morning, set out for Errol Dam for a spot of mail-collecting and shopping. At the confluence of the Androscoggin and the Magalloway his boat fell in behind the boat of a stranger, en route to the dam from points north. Phil arrived a moment behind the other, tied up at the landing and climbed the bank. The stranger was standing by the roadside in a daze.

"Hey," he said feebly. "Do you see what I see?"

Phil looked. "That isn't your car, I hope?" he asked without conviction.

"Yeah. And I was planning to hop in it and drive home to Massachusetts."

The car was neatly blocked up on four blocks. All four wheels had been removed and spirited away.

"And I had new rubber all around," the stranger announced pitifully.

I do not hold with thievery under any conditions, not even Robin Hood conditions, where the oppressed were supposed to have benefited—and, incidentally, I've always had my fingers crossed on that one. But thievery in this country is unpardonable. The few things we have here, we need. At best, having them stolen means downright inconvenience. At worst, it means suffering and possibly death. I'll string along with Phil and Ralph and underwrite their verdict: shooting's too good for a thief here. Let me get my hands on the so-and-so.

We don't see quite so much of Jessie Potter as we do of the Hesseltines, because she lives way down the lake, around the bend, on a farm, but she's one of those people whom you don't have to see very often to feel en rapport. You always take right up where you left off last time, whether last time was yesterday or a year ago. It's a very comforting feeling to know that Jessie is going to be exactly as she was when you parted. I think perhaps this is because she doesn't own a pose to her name, so she doesn't get mixed up and go into her Society Act, forgetting that three weeks ago she was being the Lady Farmer. She's always just Jessie Potter, thank heaven. She it is who has convinced me that growing older can be fun. I don't know how old she is, but she is a grandmother, for what that's worth. She's kept her figure and her looks and her sense of humor. No lavender shawls and lace caps for Jessie. Jessie gets an enormous kick out of life, and those aspects of life—such as the Riches and the Hesseltines —that come in contact with her get an enormous kick out of Jessie. It was she who came to call on me one evening, since she was going by Pine Point, anyhow, on her way back from the Outside.

"And where are the children and Catherine?" she asked politely, sitting there in her best hat and her trim, Outside suit, looking like Park Avenue.

"Oh, they're in Upton. School started last week, you know."

"And what will you and Ralph be doing this winter? Will you be with them?"

I said no, we'd be back at Forest Lodge.

"Just the two of you? Alone up there in the woods all winter?"

I said yes, that was the idea.

Jessie rose briskly and started drawing on her gloves. "I wonder if you'd ask Kenneth to bring the boat around. I think I'd better go right home and start knitting tiny garments." That's the kind of oblique retort of which she is past mistress.

And what do we do at Pine Point besides scuttle back and forth across the lake chinning with the neighbors? Well, that would be hard to say. We swim. We read and sun-bathe. We entertain our friends. We talk almost continually, since all of us and all of our friends are far from strong, silent types. We're all very vocal. It was once said of us, "They're Great Talkers over there," and it's true. This doesn't mean the same as great conversationalists. We don't converse. We just talk, intoxicated by the sound of our own voices. We get into frightful arguments about writing and cooking and politics and the proper discipline of children. We have a good time.

And believe it or not, we work; and believe it or not, we have a good time at that, too. Last summer we had in hand a big project, the laying of new boat ways for the launching of the *Puss*, which was high and dry in the winter boathouse. She had to be caulked and painted first, and since we had that unspeakable Chris-craft to run about in, there seemed to be no great rush about putting the *Puss* into the water. But by the time she was ready to launch, they'd lowered the lake so much, because of work that must be done on Errol Dam, that the ways had to be extended eighteen feet.

All hands, which included Ralph, Doc Stuart and Whit Roberts, who were working for us, a boy named Frank Simmons who was staying with us, Stark Hesseltine from across the lake, my editor, George Stevens, who was visiting us, and Catherine and I assembled. It didn't look like too hard a job, we decided. All we had to do was extend the present length of iron rail with a couple of lengths more, which we had on hand. Working together and largely under water, we could get them in place and spike them down to some sunken boom logs which were already laid. Nothing to it at all. Or that's what we thought.

And weren't we wrong! The boom logs, we discovered at once to our sorrow, were weighted at the ends with an old bateau full of rocks, which itself was spiked in place. The whole thing was waterlogged, and lay in six feet of water. We had to remove it before we could get our rails down. It couldn't be done, said Ralph, Doc, and Whit.

Catherine and I exchanged glances. "Nuts!" we said silently to each other, and dove in. Certainly it could be done, and the first step was to unload the rocks from the bateau.

Have you ever unloaded fifty rocks, the smallest the size of your head, from a boat six feet under water? It's not what it's cracked up to be. They lift fairly easily, buoyed up as they are, but you're working on the bottom without benefit of diver's helmet. If you keep your eyes open, they shortly begin to smart and redden. If you close your eyes you can't see what you're doing, and chances are that you and someone else are hauling, with bursting lungs, on the same rock in opposite directions. It took Frank and Stark and Catherine and me two days to unload that boat. The second day was the worst for Catherine and me. By that time her son Vaughn and my son Rufus had begun to take an active interest in proceedings, and every time we came up for air would shout helpfully from the float where they were hopping about excitedly, "Ooh, Mamma! Look! I see a bloodsucker! Ooh, Mamma, he's a *huge* one and he's coming right for you!" We loved that.

The third day we started to pry the bateau loose, only to discover that it was wired down, as well as spiked. We cut the wire. Then we tried to pull the spikes. They were rusted in firmly, and we ourselves were too buoyant to get a decent purchase under water. Catherine and I tried to saw them off with a hacksaw, but it was no use. Finally we retired to the shore and held a consultation of war. She and I had brashly announced we'd get that thing out of there, everyone was waiting smugly for us to give up, and we'd be damned if we would.

"I'll go up and tell Doris what to get for lunch," Catherine

said—Doris was a little refugee girl who was staying with us—
"and then we'll look the situation over."

Looking the situation over consisted of Catherine's dis-
appearing under water with a final injunction for me to keep
my foot on her neck until she slapped my ankle. She could
hold her breath but she couldn't overcome her buoyancy.
I don't know who suffered more on those reconnoitering
expeditions. She couldn't have enjoyed being held down
like that, and I'm sure I didn't enjoy holding her. After
what seemed like half an hour to me—but was actually about
thirty seconds—I'd begin to wonder if she'd quietly
drowned, without strength enough to slap. So I'd let her
up. She'd come to the surface sputtering, "Hey! I was just
beginning to find things out!" And down she'd go again.
She finally concluded we'd have to tear the bateau to pieces
to get it out, and that was the program for the next day.

That night hell began to pop. We were all sitting in the
living-room, reading—and talking—when the lights blazed,
flickered, and dimmed. Ralph rushed to the powerhouse and
found that the Kohler had thrown the fan belt and was
running red hot. He threw the switch and we were in darkness. We dug up some candles and lamps and finished the
evening in a picturesque gloom. I finally said I guessed I'd
take a hot shower and go to bed.

"For God's sake, no!" Ralph howled. "The pump won't
work without the Kohler. If you pull the pressure down, the
coils in the stove will go dry and you can't build a fire without burning out the water front. Put signs on all the faucets.
No one is to draw any water or use the bathroom until the
pump is running again." So we all went down to the lake to
wash our faces and brush our teeth. We were back to funda-
mental principles. Fortunately the weather was superb and

the water warm, so no one really suffered; and anyhow, there were northern lights that night which we wouldn't have seen if the Kohler hadn't folded. It could have been worse.

It shortly became worse. In the middle of breakfast-preparations the grate fell out of the kitchen stove, dumping the fire and filling the place with smoke too dense to be endured. We finished cooking breakfast over the living-room fireplace—a process that sounds like a lot more fun than it is. Then we took turns lugging pails of water from the lake for the dishwashing, and Ralph propped up the, now, cold grate with a couple of bricks, an expedient which he thought would serve for a day or two. It's still serving, eighteen months later. It collapses every now and then, and we say, "We *must* get this damn grate fixed." But so far we never think of it at the right times. You know how it is.

After breakfast, and before we started our submarine operations, Ralph decided we'd better run over to Hessel-tines' with Whit and Doc, and fix their flagpole, which was down. It was a four-man job, and we'd said we'd help do it. Better get that out of the way before becoming involved in a major affair. The four of us boarded the Chris-craft and set off with a flourish. Much as I hate the Chris-craft, I will admit it is a stylish boat. You zoop across the lake, flinging wide, white wings of water right and left, and feeling like something out of *Yachting* or a Coca-Cola advertisement.

This was a feeling that was soon dispelled. Just off Hes-seltines' float we halted with a terrifying, grinding crash, which certainly could mean only one thing. We'd run onto a reef and ripped the bottom out of her. Doc and I began to tear up floor boards like mad, and desisted only when it became apparent that she wasn't taking in any water.

Ralph started up the motor again, and the most horrible clatter ensued as we advanced at a pace which would have shamed even an old-lady snail. "Shaft," said Ralph grimly. "Jesus. She must be bent all to hell." He sighed deeply. "You know, Babe, I'm rather relieved. Now everything possible has happened to us, so we can relax. Everything, that is, except a forest fire."

I crossed my fingers and overlooked the "Babe." I hate to be called Babe, but it seemed to me to be no time to Take Issue. I retaliated feebly by saying, "Smile when you say 'forest fire,' Bud." Ralph hated me to call him "Bud."

We landed, fixed the flagpole, and took what slim comfort we could out of Phil's assurance that we'd cleverly discovered an entirely new ledge that no one had ever known about before, which had come to the surface only because of the unprecedented lowness of the lake. Then we limped sadly home. Ralph, Whit, and Doc slung up the Chris-craft in the wet boathouse and started taking out the shaft, which would have to be sent Outside to be straightened. I lowered the flag to half-mast, at Ralph's request, and Catherine and I set again to work on our way-laying stint. It was outside the realm of the sporting venture now. Now we had no boat at all. We *had* to get the *Puss* into the water, or depend entirely upon canoes. Canoes are fine, but not for hauling freight and groceries for twenty people, four miles; and not for the kind of heavy sea that Umbagog could, and most certainly would, kick up the minute someone broke an arm and had to be taken to the doctor.

Thank God the weather was hot and the sun, bright. If we'd had to work in a bone-chilling drizzle, I don't know how any of us—Catherine or George or Frank or Stark or I—could have stood an eight-hour day of parboiling. Catherine was the Engineer In Charge. She'd go down, fix the hooks of cant dogs at strategic points, and come up with the order to pry. We'd all pry. At intervals something would give way and we'd all flop into the lake, closing the door behind us. Then we'd come up and do it again. We swore like stevedores and then laughed like fools, to the detriment of our prying ability but to the benefit of our morale. The kids continued their good work as bloodsucker-spotters, but we no longer cared. The game warden, Leon Wilson, dropped in and made fun of us, sitting maddeningly neat and dry on the float and smoking cigarettes. We discussed pitching him into the drink, just for instance, but didn't have time to do it. We'd fix him later. Pearl Cushman, known hereabouts as "that red-haired secretary of Louise's," came down to ask about some ambiguous punctuation in a manuscript she was typing for me and remained to take pictures. Catherine and I knew we looked like the Wrath-to-Come, but we didn't even bother to swipe back our damp and stringy hair. We were past being camera conscious. Whit walked out on a stringer to see how things were coming, and I spoke to him over my shoulder, which was on a level with his feet. I looked back to what I was doing, glanced up again to ask him a question, and found only bland blue sky. Startled, I looked around. He was swimming placidly ashore, having fallen into the lake. The whole thing was a madhouse, in which it was perfectly normal for a man of over sixty to paddle about in Umbagog completely clothed, smoking a cigarette, with his hat still neat and level over his brows. I didn't even laugh. I went back to work.

At noon we knocked off for the lunch Doris had prepared —corned beef and cabbage—a departure for a little Austrian, I would think—which we ate in our dripping deep-sea clothes. Catherine and I had decided, days before, that we weren't going to ruin our good and only bathing suits grubbing around rusty rails, so we'd donned ancient shorts, old halters, and worn sneakers. We looked awful. My own aplomb was not increased by a general verdict that if I spent one more day in the water, I wouldn't be decent. The seat of my pants was tissue-paper thin.

At twelve-thirty we went back to work—and I mean work. We pried. We hauled. We defied all recognized laws of aquatics, gravity, and displacement. And then, suddenly and undramatically, at two-five sharp, that damn bateau gave up the ghost and floated free. We would have cheered, had we had the necessary breath. As it was, we simply swam her out to sea and let her sink. R.I.P.

"Now," said Ralph, "we'll lay the rails." The fact that he was interrupting a mutually congratulatory congress between Catherine and me seemed unimportant. We laid the rails.

Did you ever try to spike down ten-foot rails in six feet of water? Take it from one who knows, and don't. Nothing is so unwieldy as a sledge hammer under water. You know what you're doing, but you don't do it. You see what you're hitting, but you don't hit it. It's like one of those dreams of childhood, in which you struggle and struggle and get nowhere. Finally Whit evolved a system whereby one drove the spikes in the open air, through a pipe. That worked. We got the double-damned, blue bottomed, jumped-up, jeesley rails laid. First thing to-morrow morning, we'd launch the *Puss*. In the meantime, Ralph would see about getting the Kohler started. And I would change my clothes, which were, frankly, rotting on me.

I cold-creamed my face. I took a cake of soap and went

down to the float—having warned all away—and had a nice sudsy bath. I put on a white silk shirt and green corduroy pants. I debated between pearl earrings—synthetic—and emeralds—also synthetic. I filed my nails to cattish points and painted them an interesting color called "Autumn Tulip." I found *Lady Chatterley's Lover* in Mr. Leman's bookcase and decided I owed it to myself to read it. I stretched out, as nearly beautiful as the Lord will allow Louise, in a deck chair on the porch, my hair piled high and dignified. Brother, I was Something, don't let anybody tell you different. I fancied myself.

But not for long. Ralph came onto the porch, and I greeted him with a Mme. Pompadour glance which he ignored. "Babe," he said, "I hate to ask you, but would you give me a hand? I've ground the valves down, and I can't get the damn cones back in place. My fingers are too big. Would you——"

I groaned and gave Autumn Tulip a fond, valedictory look. I knew what portended. I'd been mechanic's helper before. I'm a bum mechanic but I'm a swell mechanic's helper. I don't know a damn thing, so all I can do is follow orders explicitly, a prime requisite in a helper. Then if the Boss gets stuck and asks for advice, I give it. I'm so simple that the rules of the game are completely unknown to me. I'm not hidebound. I say, "I think maybe if we did thus and so——" not knowing that my program is contrary to Hoyle. More often than not, my silly suggestions work.

I said to Ralph once, "I think maybe I'll go somewhere and take a six-weeks' course in gasoline motors. Then I could really be a help to you."

He said, "Jesus, Babe, *no*! There's nothing like having an unorthodox, virgin mind on the premises. Promise me, seriously, that you'll keep your brain a blank, as far as motors go."

So I promised, and I've kept my promise. I'm the Kallikaks' little sister in the field of combustion.

I went down to the pumphouse and viewed the valves. Some little bisected cones had to be placed around a spindle —I don't even know the proper names for these things— under a stiff spring. The spring was held up by a contraption called a valve-spreader. I rolled up my sleeves, kissed my nail enamel good-bye, and set to work, with a final injunction that Ralph would not, by all the saints, let the spreader slip. Even I could see that that was an easy way to lose a finger.

Of all the exasperating, fiddling jobs! I'd just get one piece in place and start on the other, when one of us would think a slightly rugged thought, and piece Number One would drop off into the grease pan. That's how sensitive the operation was. I'd carefully restrain myself from violent language—it does no good, I have found, to lose your temper with a mass of steel—and start all over again.

Finally I said, "This needs a special tool, and I'm going to make one." I snatched a hairpin out of my head, bent it into a lower-case *y*-shape, and went on from there. Ralph retched, and I said a bit acidly, "What ails you, Bud?"

He said, "I'm a fool. But I hate to see a piece of good masculine machinery at the mercy of a woman. Then when you use a hairpin on it—I'm sorry, Babe, but it's insulting and revolting."

Do all men feel that way about motors, machines, and engines? If they do, they're even more sentimental than I thought.

We got the thing fixed. That night we had light and water,

and we sat about in comfort, discussing the launching of the *Puss,* which was to take place the next morning.

"We'll get the *Puss* into the water," we said. "The light plant is fixed. The stove works. To-morrow night the shaft for the Chris-craft will come in and we'll get her going. Then we can raise the flag to full mast. Everything has happened to us," we said. "We've got nothing more to worry about."

The next day, half an hour after the *Puss* was launched and long before we got the shaft back, the Forest Fire started!

CHAPTER VI

The Forest Fire

I HAD ARISEN at five-thirty, a thing I frequently do in summer—to the amazement of all who know me—for three reasons, the first of which is that since I start writing at nine or thereabouts and continue until one, any little chore that I have on my mind to do in the morning must be done early. The second is that I like to swim before breakfast, and unless I get my licks in before anyone else is circulating around, I have to wear a bathing suit, oh, hideous thought.

Umbagog is wonderful in the morning. It is so shallow that by the middle of August the water is warm and soft and silky from the heat of the summer sun, and when the air chills at night with the first hint of autumn, the lake steams gently through the hours of darkness. By morning a dense blanket of fog lies over it, a blanket only about twenty feet thick. It's fascinating to climb up onto the roof of Pine Point and find yourself in a pure, clear, sun-drenched world. The tops of the trees about the lake are thrust up through the fog like islands, into the level golden light, and the mountains, sharp and purple, stand about the sea of billowing mother-of-pearl. The flag hangs limp on its fog-based staff, a shout of color against the bright blue of the sky. You lean against the chimney for a long moment and wonder if anything, anywhere, was ever so spectacularly beautiful. Then you climb back down the ladder into the no less lovely world below, a world whose beauty is luminous and hazy and subtle, where all objects possess the soft quality of dreams, their outlines blurred, their colors muted.

In fairness I must admit that this late-summer and early-autumn morning fog has its disadvantages if you want to go somewhere in a hurry. Unless you are much better acquainted with the lake than we are, you'd better stay at home until the fog lifts. Before Ralph and I learned that, we set out once in the *Puss* for Sunday Cove, intending to run up to Middle Dam for our mail and get back by nine o'clock. The minute we got out of the Cove where the wet boathouse rides at anchor, we were flying blind. We took a big swoop to the west and north, and proceeded at half speed for about twenty minutes, with all the confidence of ignorance. Then I glanced over the side. "Say," I asked, "should we be running through eelgrass?"

Ralph killed the motor hastily. "Jesus, no." He plunged a pickpole over the side into about three feet of water. The *Puss* draws about three feet of water. "Now where in hell are we?"

"The only eelgrass I know is over by Moose Point. We can't be there, can we? Or can we?"

"God only knows." He poled slowly back until we were in deep water again. We still could see nothing. "We must be, though. In that case Sunday Cove is right over there." He pointed into the fog.

"Yep," I agreed, "right over there." He started the engine again and we nosed into the dimness in a very gingerly manner. I took soundings with the pickpole every few yards, and shortly discovered bottom again at four feet. "Must have clipped her too close. A little more to the right," I suggested.

"Starboard," he corrected, shutting off the engine and poling again. "Keep your vocabulary clean, Babe." He started the motor and we proceeded until we ran aground. "Hell," he said simply, "now we're over by Cliff's."

"Then Sunday Cove is right over there," I announced, pointing.

"Yep, right over there," he agreed. We still had seen nothing more solid than a leaf floating, nothing but the thick gray of the fog.

I won't bore you with details of the next two hours, since it would be simple repetition. We poled, we proceeded at the lowest speed, we stopped and poled, then we'd drift awhile and smoke and talk. Then we'd proceed at low speed. Finally we agreed that we were certainly lying off the entrance of the Cove, and since it was a bit narrow and difficult, we'd better wait there until the fog lifted. We weren't losing our courage, but we were getting a little sense. We dropped anchor and took advantage of the pause to pump out the bilge and clean the gas line, two chores that needed doing.

At eleven o'clock the fog started thinning and we could see a faint outline of shore. "Look!" said Ralph. "There's someone sitting on a rock! Let's ask them——"

We weighed anchor and edged in toward shore. "Ahoy!" Ralph hailed, determinedly nautical, and the person on the rock jumped to his feet and barked delightedly. "Kyak, you damned fool!" said Ralph. "How in blazes did you get way over here?"

The sun shot suddenly through the murk—it's amazing how quickly the fog dissipates once the sun is high enough to warm the air—and Ralph and I stood gaping. The rock

Kyak was sitting on was the rock by the flagpole, less than thirty feet from the porch of the house. We were right back where we'd started from, four hours before.

"Have a nice trip, Mrs. Rich?" Ralph asked sardonically, and we went ashore and cooked lunch.

But the morning of the launching of the *Puss* no one wanted to go anywhere, so I had a swell swim, marred by only one contretemps: I was loafing along about fifty feet from shore, thinking my own thoughts and doing no harm, when a boat loomed suddenly out of the fog. It was Cliff, bound on some errand the nature of which I never did find out, since I pretended I didn't see him and he—although he nearly ran me down—pretended he didn't see me. Cliff is a gentleman. I went ashore, investigated the muskrat nest under the float, discovered that the repeated attentions of the children had not yet frightened the mother and four young away, and returned to the house for breakfast. That's the third reason I like to get up early. I can eat what I want for breakfast without being sneered at, since Catherine is the only one around and she likes the same kind of break- fast that I do. We had orange juice, tomato, cucumber and lettuce sandwiches, and coffee. I might as well admit that sometimes we have been known to have tuna fish salad, sometimes cold spinach and French dressing with stuffed celery, and once a shrimp cocktail. Otherwise broadminded people take a very reactionary stand about what is per- missible to eat for breakfast, and while I figure that that is strictly my own business, still and all, it saves a lot of talk if I eat mine in private.

The first thing we did, as soon as all hands were on deck, was put the *Puss* into the water. She slid down our new ways like a lady, and within fifteen minutes we tied up at the float.

Then we decided that since we'd spent most of the week in the lake, laying those same ways, we'd get caught up on a few things. Whit, Doc, and Ralph were going to burn a little brush down on the rocks by the shore before the fog wore off, so the lookouts on the mountains wouldn't see the smoke and get all hot and bothered about it. Then as soon as it was clear, Ralph was going to Middle Dam. No one had been there for a long time and we had mail and groceries to collect, and a whole list of errands to do. I took from the empty shell case on the living-room table all the little slips of paper on which people had been making notes of needs during the past week, and started setting them down.

Those lists were always something. That's one of the penalties of living in three places at once. Half the things you want are always—if you are at Pine Point—either at Forest Lodge or in whatever village, such as Upton, the children are currently attending school. No matter how carefully you pack to move, you always forget something, or some unexpected situation arises requiring unthought-of equipment. I kept that list, for some unfathomable reason, and it is a very fair example of what I mean. Here it is:

List for Ralph

> Vaughn's jacket on hook in kitchen
> See Larry about case of eggs on Friday
> L's old bathing-cap in the bureau drawer
> C's knitting in living-room
> 1 doz. cans tomato soup
> Ask Skinny if Pearl's slacks are done at cleaners
> 50¢ dog food
> 2 cans lye
> 1 sheet 3c stamps
> Typewriter ribbon in desk

Pick cucumbers
Rufus orange truck on porch
See if Pearsons are still here, and if so leave word Louise wants
  to see Ann
Ask Mrs. Roberts for crochet bedspread instructions
Ask Skinny to get nec. amt. crochet cotton
Large double-boiler

I just said to Pearl, "For crying out loud, Pearl, what does this mean? *Real passion,* indeed!" and she had looked over my shoulder at the slip I was trying to decipher—she'd written it—and said, "Oh! *Rat poison,* of course," when the telephone rang.

It was Joe Mooney, over at the Brown Farm. "Hey, Louise," he said. "Do you see anything of any smoke over by Sturtevant Cove? We just had a report on a forest fire over there."

"Oh Lord, Joe," I advised him blandly. "Don't give it a thought. That's just us burning brush down on the rocks. Everything's under control."

"Well, that's good." He sounded relieved. "Only, Louise, you'd ought to call us up before you start a fire. You're not supposed to start fires without notifying the warden service."

"Well, you know it now," I said, and asked a bit tardily, "Is it all right?"

"God, no. After the weather we been having? It hasn't rained for thirty-three days, and the temperature hasn't been below eighty. Where have you been?"

"In the lake," I told him and left him to make what he could out of that. "I'll go tell them to put the fire out right away."

"You do that. There's a hell of a fire up to Kennebago—already burned over five thousand acres, and no sign of controlling it yet. They got two thousand men up there, fighting. We don't want no fires here. Wouldn't be anyone to fight it."

"Why don't they slap on a band?" I asked, relapsing into the patois. After a prolonged period of drought, when the danger of forest fire is very great, the governor of the State issues a proclamation closing the woods to any except wardens and persons who live there. It forbids fishing, camping, building fires, and smoking, to anyone at all, even wardens. The woods are banned to the public—or as we say, "a band is slapped on." "Anyhow, Joe, I'll see the fire is put out."

I went down to the shore and delivered my message. The fire was almost out, anyhow, since the fog had lifted, and a few pails of water finished up the job. I stopped on the way back to admire the *Puss,* fresh in her new paint. She certainly looked handsome with her clean white hull, her bright blue decks, and her dazzling brass, I thought. If Ralph thinks he's going to mess her all up with that filthy cultch he's always carting around, I told myself with more optimism than conviction, he's mistaken. Let him build a scow for his junk. Then I crossed the Point to the pump-house float for the purpose of admiring the view—and stopped short. In the direction of Sturtevant Cove, a mile up and across the lake, a towering column of smoke pillowed up two hundred yards. I started back to the house on the run, and cranked the "two long" that would put Joe on the line.

"Joe, I was all wet about the fire. There is one at Sturtevant Cove. Can't tell from here how big, but there's an awful lot of smoke." I didn't add that I felt responsible, to a degree, nor why.

But the truth of the matter was that the evening before, when we all—the household and the Stevenses and the Edsons, who were our guests—were sitting around the living-room, Doc Stuart had come in, in more or less of a dither. "I've just been out paddling around in a canoe, and I saw a fire over on the New Hampshire side. We'd ought to do something about it."

Well, if there really was a fire, of course we'd ought to do something about it; but it seemed improbable that none of the New Hampshire-side people had noticed it. And besides, we were comfortable. Catherine was writing letters, George Stevens was working out astronomical problems for his own amusement—he'd found a book on astronomy in the bookcase and taken the heavens to his heart—Ralph was studying Sears' catalogue, and the rest of us were playing a game of our own invention. It consisted of each reading an advertisement heading from a magazine and calling upon the others in turn to guess what product was being promoted. This is a pretty simple pastime for adults, but it's worth trying. It demonstrates effectively the depths of asininity to which an advertising copy writer's mind will fall. Does "To a Pioneer" introduce a better and bigger bowie knife? Oh my, no! It's trying to sell you the idea of a green lipstick. Does "It makes a Heavenly Harmony" refer to a musical instrument? Don't be naïve, Pet, or you'll be buying good sensible flat-heeled shoes under the impression you're purchasing a piano. A variation of this game consists of cutting out newspaper photographs and hounding your housemates with the query, "Why did this person get his picture into the paper?" It's then that you will discover that ministers look like murderers, and in-

surance-poisoners look like women's club presidents. However——

On this occasion my sense of civic responsibility tri-
umphed and I told Doc I'd paddle over to the New Hampshire side with him to investigate. We set out in the canoe
dedicated to his personal use, since he had repaired it and
painted it a bright orange on his own time. It was a calm
and lovely night, moonless but clear, with the stars near
enough to grasp and their reflections as bright and palpable
as gold sequins on the smooth black satin of the water. We
rounded the Point, and there was nothing to be seen but the
star-spangled sky and water and the dark New Hampshire
shore line, a mile away.

"Look," I said, "you're crazy. What you saw was a light
over in the priests' camp. They've gone to bed now. There's
no sense in our paddling 'way over there."

So we didn't, but I guess he had seen a fire, which by the
time we went to look again had been damped down by the
evening dew, as is the way with incipient forest fires. At any
rate, now there really was a fire, and no fooling.

I don't know whether I can make it clear to you the horror
even the thought of forest fire strikes to the heart of the
forest dweller. It's not only that you, personally, and your
home and family and all your possessions, are in actual
danger of annihilation. That is true of a city dweller who
knows there is a fire in his block. It's more than that. It's
the knowledge that trees which took decades to grow to
beauty and dignity are dying in agony; that the deer and
bear and wildcats and rabbits—even the little deer mice—
are running, running, running in blind terror, to fall exhausted and to be consumed; that the element which is as
natural to us as air and water, the silent, green, cool endless

woods, is being destroyed; that after the fire has passed there will be nothing but the scorched earth, black and ugly, studded with the charred skeletons of once magnificent trees and crossed with parched gullies where once flowed icy streams.

That is why, the minute we knew there really was a fire, we, along with everyone else within a radius of twenty miles, dropped everything and started getting ready to go. One of our guests said, "But why are we all getting excited? It's over the other side of the lake. It isn't *our* fire." The answer to that is that any fire in the woods is everybody's fire.

Already we could see signs of fevered activity—Jessie Potter's *Bootlegger* with three house guests, her two farmers, and her chauffeur Kenneth aboard, and Ken Hinckley's kicker with three men from Upton in it tearing up the lake; the Brown Company's steel tender with a crew of about fifteen nosing out of the narrow channel of the Androscoggin; the red State plane circling from the northern sky to drop light as an autumn leaf on the water. Ralph, Whit, Doc, Frank, Stark—who was on one of his four-day calls on us at the time—and George Stevens and Ru Edson—our guests— piled aboard the *Puss,* armed with cant dogs and axes, and set out, while we assorted wives and loved ones stood on the float waving and shouting such helpful last minute words as "Now be careful!" and "Don't get hurt!" We were treated with the contempt which we deserved. Then we sat down to wait as befitted ladies, although we'd all much rather have been at the fire. We could see just enough of it to drive us crazy—boats skittering back and forth, the plane rising, circling, and then arrowing away toward parts unknown only to return in a few minutes, and sudden flares of orange flame or great black bursts of smoke—but we couldn't see enough to tell us whether we were winning or losing. We didn't know whether to start planning the kind of celebration returned heroes deserve—which meant opening the one jar of caviar I'd been saving for six years to serve with the even older bottle of Scotch, and putting in to roast the chickens we'd consecrated to the morrow—or whether to begin packing the more valuable of our possessions and rounding up the smaller children so we could lay hand on them when we had to flee.

Then we saw the *Puss* detach herself from the scene and start toward home, with only Ralph aboard. He'd been sent, it developed in due course, to get ten gallons of gasoline for the portable pump motor which had been flown down from Cupsuptic and set up on the shore to feed the two-hundred-foot hose lines running up into the woods.

Dorothy Edson and Laura Stevens asked simultaneously, as soon as Ralph was within loud-shouting distance, "Is Ru—George—all right?" and I asked, "Are Frank and Stark all right, because after all I'm *in loco matri*"—or words to that effect. Ralph said they all were, and then, bless his heart, added to me, "Get aboard, Babe, if you want to come with me." If I wanted to come with him, for Pete's sake!

I said, "Wait a minute till I change my clothes. I'm not dressed for a forest fire"—I was wearing too-short shorts and too halting a halter—and he said, "For the love of God! I can't wait! Come as you are or not at all." Then he relented. "There's that old slicker that got paint spilled on it in the cabin. You can wear that if it gets too hot." It didn't occur to me that there was anything odd in wearing a raincoat to a forest fire, so I got aboard.

It was my first, last, and only forest fire and I had the time

of my life. So that I won't be put down as a completely
feather-headed fool—and in view of what I have just said
about the gravity of fire in the forest—let me hasten to explain that by the time I got to the scene, the fire was well under control, there was no danger of any great damage being
done, and only about twenty acres had been burned off. As
fires go, that was nothing. The blaze had started well out
toward the end of a point. What light breeze stirred was
from the west, toward the lake, so the fire could advance
only very slowly against it, in spite of the tinder dryness of
the woods. Fighting the fire consisted mainly of confining it
to the point and letting it burn itself out there. This was
accomplished by swamping out and soaking a swath across
the base of the point and keeping watch that any sparks
which jumped the swath should immediately be extinguished. The long hose lines from the shore pump played
along the front of the fire, and men armed with shovels or
Indian pumps patrolled the swath. An Indian pump, in
case you didn't know, is a portable tank, with straps like a
knapsack, which a man carries on his back. Attached to it is
a short length of hose. You fill it with water from the lake,
run back to the fire, squirt the water around where it will
do the most good until the tank is empty, and then start all
over again. It's hard work, but reasonably effective if the fire
is near a good supply of water. I noticed that George Stevens
and Ru Edson, being city slickers and too ignorant to protest, had been issued Indian pumps which they were con-
scientiously employing. This didn't surprise me at all. The
old hands, the men who had fought forest fires off and on
all their lives, could be trusted to grab shovels before anyone
could foist pumps on them. All a man with a shovel had to

do was lean on it until he saw a small blaze spring up. Then he pitched a little dirt on it, stamped it down, and went back to his meditations.

The first person I saw as the *Puss* drew into shore was Ambi Hines, the warden from the Narrows of the Richardson lakes. He was tending the shore pump, which was set up on a rickety old landing, pumping water for gosh-sake and making an ungodly clatter. That didn't dismay either Ambi or me. We hadn't seen each other for over a year and we intended to make the most of the encounter. "How's your wife?" I shrieked at the top of my lungs. "Fine. How are the kids?" he howled back. Then he came over to the boat to help Ralph unload the gas cans. "You know, Louise," he confided with an air of pride, "we got five-six sports helping fight *this* fire!" That quite definitely established *this* fire as a very toney affair, not in the class with riffraff fires like Kennebago at all. I looked properly impressed and refrained from mentioning that two of the sports in question were mine; and I'm glad I did, because he went on to say, "God, they're good workers, too. One of them's worth three woodsmen. Do what you tell them. Take it serious. Don't catch them sittin' down back of a bush smoking cigarettes." I stored that up to report to my two sports when, as, and if, I ever caught up with them. Ambi went back to his pump, but the whole tenor of the fire had been established. It was a Social Occasion.

So I felt no compunctions about hailing Ben Bennett when he came puttering up in his outboard and drew alongside the *Puss*. "Ain't seen you since God wore knee-britches," he told me. "Last time I see you, met you on the carry, bird hunting three years ago. Old Cliff wanted me to tell you, case I run into you over here, come over to his place to-morrow and he'd give you what string beans you can pick."

"You tell old Cliff thank-you, I will," I said. Ben and Cliff always refer to each other patronizingly as "old" or sometimes in extremity "poor old." I doubt if there is six months difference in their ages. They're both well over seventy. "Quite a fire," I added, feeling that after all the fire should have at least a token recognition.

He glanced over his shoulder at the holocaust, apparently decided it wasn't worth mentioning, looked again and asked, "Ain't that Doc Stuart comin' out the woods? What in hell's he doing here?"

"Fighting fire," I said pointedly. "He's working for us this summer."

"I'll be God damned. Ain't laid eyes on Doc for twenty years. Hey, Doc!"

Doc looked, stopped short, abandoned whatever mission he was on, and climbed into the *Puss*. "Christ-in-the-foot-hills, you old son of a sea-going bob-cat, last time I see you was that fracas at Nat Leach's, spring we come off the Magalloway drive. God-a'mighty, you don't look a day older. Say, remember how you busted the bottle over that varmint's head from Parmachene——"

They were off. I turned my attention to the shore activities. The State plane was just making a landing and coasting in to the beach. Two woodsmen waded out, knee deep, and babied the crate in. She rode high and light on her pontoons, but she still wasn't anything to write home about—only a motor, a pair of wings, and an open cockpit. Crate was the word for her, and I don't mean maybe.

Now I have always had my illusions about aviators, and I've had ideas about warden services. In my book, aviators and wardens are always neat, clean, trim, and in uniform. Of course, I'd just been shooting the breeze with Ambi, and he'd had on a dirty shirt and denim pants, and his face was smeared with grease, but that was different. He was an old acquaintance. He was allowed leeway. When it came down to a stranger flying the plane of the sovereign State of Maine, I expected socks and a necktie. What I got was a young man by the name of Miller wearing an unbuttoned shirt, nondescript pants, and moccasins with no socks. Before the plane was safely beached he jumped overside, kicked off his foot gear, and sat down with his feet in the water. His face was smudged, his hair was all over his head, and he looked harassed. But I didn't have any more attention to spare for him, I'd just noticed a certain familiar something about one of the woodsmen who had towed the plane in. He looked like—he was!—my favorite Wes Farris.

"Hey, Wes!" I shouted, turning my back on Doc's and Ben's conversation, which had reached the point of "sure you know who he is. Why, his uncle swapped dogs with your cousin Ed in 1919. You remember that spotted hound."

Wes turned around slowly. "Missus!" he exclaimed with every appearance of pleasure. "Jesus to Jesus and three hands 'round. I ain't seen you since a year ago last spring, down to the comp'ny wangan in Errol. You're lookin' good. Put on a little weight, ain't you?"

I admitted the gentle impeachment and asked him if he'd seen Bill Lace lately. "See him not more'n ten minutes ago. He's up back"—he jerked a thumb in the general direction of the fire—"on the hose line. You ain't got a match on you, have you, Missus? I been wantin' to smoke for the last hour."

Considering the fact that the world was in flame about him, I couldn't quite follow why he needed a match, if he really wanted to smoke; but I concluded it was a fixation of some sort and gave him one. He thanked me, we made a date to go horn-pouting a week from Sunday, when, he assured me, he'd return the match, and he sauntered back to the plane. Miller had his moccasins on again and was about to take off for Cupsuptic, to get the head warden. He taxied her carefully away from shore, revved her up, and lifted her into the air. He may have looked like the tail end of a mis-spent Fourth of July, but that boy could certainly fly. He circled the fire once, low, peering anxiously over the edge of the cockpit, and then streaked off northward. I looked around to see what had become of Ralph and discovered him in conference with Gordon Bragg.

"Hi, Gordon," I said. "How's Kay? How's the kid?"

"Fine. Haven't seen you since that day you gave the kid the stuffed owl, two years ago. Kay's still sore at you. The kid raises hell if he can't take it to bed and the damn thing sheds and has moths." I made appropriate and insincere, regret-ful sounds. I hadn't cared for the owl either.

The plane hove in sight again over the ridge, circled the fire, drifted like a feather to the surface of the lake, and loafed up to the beach. Miller jumped out, kicked off his moccasins, and thrust his feet into the water. "Don't tell me," I said to Ralph, "he's been to Cupsuptic! He's only been gone twenty minutes." "Must have been. There's Harold York with him." I was speechless. I'd been to Cupsuptic too, on the whirl around the lakes. I went the regular way, the hard way. I went by canoe and it took two days of dogged paddling. I felt a slight resentment toward Miller. He didn't have blisters on his hands and a crick in his back, as I'd had. No, all he had was a phobia about soaking his feet.

Harold York joined us. "How are you, Ralph? Just been

to Kennebago this morning. Hell of a fire up there. The Canadian services have sent down five hundred men to fight it, but unless we get rain, nothing's going to stop it short of Hudson Bay. God damn a forest fire."

"How's this one coming?" Ralph asked. At a forest fire, even if you are paying attention to the fire and not to Old Home Week, as we were, you can't tell how it's going. It's like a big battle. All you know is what's happening in your immediate sector. Harold York had seen it from the air. He should know.

"All right. Nothing to it now. Soon's the sun sets and the dew commences falling, all we'll need is a couple of men to watch her. This is a good fire."

"Well," I said to Ralph, "how about taking me up into the woods so I can view this 'good fire?' After all, I haven't even seen it yet, not really. All I've seen is smoke and some burned trees along the shore. Wait till I get my slicker—" I didn't think it necessary to explain to Harold York that the idea of the slicker was not to keep dry, but to keep sparks off my bare back and arms. I had no hankering for a coal-pitted epidermis.

We walked up the path past the priests' camp—a neat little cottage built by the Catholic priests of Berlin—and into the woods, into a strange nether-worldly scene. The fire had been a quick one, stripping leaves and needles from the trees but not stopping to devour the sap-laden wood. The boles and branches rose about us and met over our heads, perfect and unconsumed, but charred a Stygian black. The ground we trod was black, too, as far as we could see. Wisps of smoke and wreaths of steam drifted among the bare trees like souls in purgatory, the souls of the trees which had died in this place. We caught brief distant glimpses of strange, misshapen creatures, dirty and tattered and haggard, plodding about this outer chamber of Hades.

Ralph and I started back to the shore, and arrived there just in time to see Miller don his moccasins and take the plane off, and Mrs. Potter's *Bootlegger* dock at the landing. "Hello, Mrs. Rich," Kenneth hailed me. "What you got in all the kettles, Kenneth?" I asked.

He started unloading them. "Lunch. Brown Comp'ny sent it up from the Pontuck wangan for their men."

I don't know how word got back into the woods so fast, but before Kenneth had half his kettles out of the boat, the entire company of professional woodsmen had assembled on the beach, started a lunch fire—turning their backs on the feature attraction of the day, the forest fire—and were settling down to the serious business of eating.

The plane swooped in again and Miller jumped out, kicked off his moccasins and plunged his feet into the water. This I thought was getting beyond reason. I left the klatsch and went over to Harold York who had just come out of the woods. "Look," I said, "not that it's any of my business and all that, but does he soak his feet at the Cupsuptic end of the run, too?" He did. "In God's name, why?" I demanded. "Has he got a complex?"

"You'd have a complex if you had to fly that thing around. It gets so damn hot it blisters the soles of your feet. The only thing that's crazy about him is taking the jalopy off the ground at all."

I was relieved to hear it, and I felt better about all those hours and miles we'd paddled to get to Cupsuptic.

"Look," he added, "the sun's about down and we've got the company crew here. No need of your people staying any longer if they don't want to. Just have them check out with me when they leave."

I passed the word along to Ralph—who was making a deal with Mrs. Potter's Kenneth to put new buoys in the narrows —and he corralled Stark and sent him up into the woods to collect the crew. They came straggling out in due course, Doc first, then Frank and Stark and George and Ru, then Whit Roberts on the tail end.

Doc gave a howl of anguish when he saw the *Puss*. "Holy cats, look at that paint job we just finished! A forest fire is a hell of a place to take a white boat!" And he was right—my lovely *Puss* that had looked so beautiful that morning was a mess—all black smudges and grease. I said, "Maybe we can wash her off," and Ralph said, "Yes, but maybe we won't. You'd ought to know by now, Babe, that the Riches can't put on dog and keep it on. Something always happens." He was right, and I knew it, so I gave up the idea right then and there, for keeps.

Harold York came down and took names and times of arrival and departure, and we started home.

"What's the idea of the roll call?" Ru wanted to know. "What difference does it make who we are?"

"Well, the State can't very well make out a pay check to the Handsome Dark Number from the Riches, can they?" I asked.

"*Pay* check! You mean we get *paid* for this? Hey, George! We get *paid*!"

"How much?" George wanted to know, and was told thirty cents an hour.

He started figuring rapidly. "We were there five hours. That's a buck and a half. Ah! You know what I'm going to do with mine?"

"Make a down payment on an Indian pump, I bet," Ralph said, peering ahead through the layers of smoke that lay like scarves over the water. "I noticed you seemed pretty much attached to yours."

George rubbed his shoulders and groaned. "Attached is the word. No. I'm going to have it framed and hang it over my desk at the office. Then they'll *have* to believe my story. Does it say State of Maine on the check? Does the voucher tell what you got it for?" We told him yes, and he relaxed in a position of abandon on the deck.

It turned out later—the next Sunday, to be exact, when Ken Hinckley brought John to visit Rufus and killed two birds with one stone by delivering the pay checks to those of our household who had fought the fire—that George and Ru, who had likewise decided to frame his check, had been gypped. The State had raised the fire-fighting pay from thirty to seventy cents an hour. They went about all afternoon saying to each other, "Why, they can't do that to us! Let's write a letter to the *Times*. It's all right to sacrifice a dollar and a half for one's honor—but I can't afford to not cash a check for three-fifty. Can you? We've been taken advantage of." They were very righteous and indignant about the whole thing.

When we finally got home from the fire the whole shebang was waiting on the dock. Catherine said supper wouldn't be for an hour because she'd thought everyone would want a swim or a bath or a shower, and a drink on the porch, which shows her to be a woman of sense. We cleaned up, each according to his preference, climbed into fresh clothes, and sat on the porch drinking the Scotch. The sun went down in the bloody haze that is peculiar to forest fire conditions, and we told and retold the incidents of the fire. Before Catherine announced dinner, we were all heroes, even I, until I said I wasn't very hungry because I'd had two pork chops, some bread and butter, a cup of coffee and a piece of apple pie and cheese at the fire. George, Ru, Whit, Doc, Ralph, Stark, and Frank looked at me. "Why, you snake in the grass!" they said coldly.

The next afternoon at about four o'clock I went down to the pumphouse float to swim. The fire was still smoking away over on the New Hampshire side, but the old zest had gone. I didn't more than glance at the fire. I knew that there were men watching it, that it might smolder on for weeks, if the weather remained hot and still, but that unless a high wind arose, it was no longer a menace. I turned my back on it for the superior attractions of just plain everyday Umbagog scenery. The water lay like glass, and even the near hills were pale and dim in the lavender heat haze. Mount Washington, which in the crisp of autumn is sharp and near enough to touch, I could just barely see, a lonely, towering, ephemeral ghost of a mountain to the south. The Hesseltines' landing danced in the vapor from the surface of the lake, and beyond it the valley of the Androscoggin stretched southwest into a strange purple curtain of light. I looked northwest toward the Peaks of the Diamond and the valley of the Magalloway, and that same eerie light enfolded them. "Smoke from the fire," I thought. "Probably we look the same from the New Hampshire side." It could be true, although it didn't seem possible. Where I was standing the sun shone soft and gold through the smoke and haze, and a cricket chirped in the grass on the shore. A muskrat swam silently along the float, the V of his wake flattening widely behind him, and out in front a fish jumped and plopped loudly back into an expanding target of concentric circles. The world held its breath.

Then I heard a faint and faraway noise like the rush of an approaching express train. At first it was no more than a tremor in the air, but it grew and grew. The light on the New Hampshire side changed from purple to an ugly muddy green, and I saw a gray wall march down the valley of the Magalloway. Lightning played about its face, and the sound of its approach grew louder and louder. Thunder rumbled, and the gray wall moved on. It enveloped the hills and engulfed the forest fire and wiped out the whole New Hampshire shore line. Now I could almost hear the individual drops of rain pelt down on New Hampshire soil, while tongues of fire darted out of heaven and licked the hills of New Hampshire; but where I stood in Maine the boards of the float were bone dry and curled with heat under my feet and the faint chirp of the cricket rang clear in the silence. The muskrat came back along the float about his business and another fish jumped, out in front. The sun still shone on Maine, and continued to shine.

It was a strange storm—just a little local cloudburst that kept me standing with my mouth open like a zany's for three minutes, and then raced away down the valley of the Androscoggin.

And of course, put out the forest fire, once and for all.

CHAPTER VII

"Louise Rich Day"

THERE IS, over to the south-southeast of us, a pond called C Pond, because it lies in the unorganized township of C and nobody had the time or energy to think up a better name for it. After all, ponds are thick as spatter in this country, and the important thing is to stick a label on each so that people will know which you're talking about when you mention one. If there were any possibility of a real estate development taking place on C Pond, I suppose the name could be changed to Lucivee Lake, or something; but there isn't, so it's just C Pond, and that's all the name it needs.

Ever since I came here, I'd been hearing about C Pond, but I never did get to go over there. It's not too far from here—only about five miles through the bush—but there was no trail and actually no reason why I should go. There was nothing there after you got there, I understood. There was a swamp at one end and a cliff at the other, and I could see swamps and cliffs nearer home than C Pond. I probably never would have seen it at all to this day, if my publisher and his wife hadn't come to visit us three summers ago.

Lynn Carrick is one of those people blessed with an abundance of energy. What's more, he loves all outdoors. He's not one to while his vacation quietly away, sitting on the porch and reading improving books. He wants action, and the Riches were the ones to provide it in this case. I was in a particularly vulnerable position, as I had just written a book about life in the Maine woods, its perils, and the methods of coping with same. The book had not yet been published, but Lynn, as my editor, had read it. You can't write a book about what a competent woodsman you are —that was implied if not stated—and then start whining about let's not go to C Pond, when the suggestion is made. You can't say, "I've never been there and I don't know the way, and anyhow, it's too far, and we might get lost or meet a bear." Not to your publisher, you can't; not if you want him to publish another book for you. So when Lynn looked at an old map we had, saw C Pond marked on it, and said, "Let's go over there to-morrow," all I could say was "Sure," and hope to Hannah we'd get there and back in one piece.

Ralph and Gerrish were very skeptical and defeatist about the whole undertaking. They pointed out that we'd have to go by compass, and since the only map we had of the territory was very inaccurate, we might easily entirely miss the pond, which isn't very large, and spend the rest of our strictly limited days wandering in a void. I offered to let them come, too, on the basis that four heads are better than one, but they just laughed at me and wanted to know if I thought they were crazy. Lynn's wife, Virginia, and my sister, Alice, said they'd go, though; and while in the beginning Ralph and Gerrish had taken the attitude that I was a licensed Maine guide and this was my expedition—so do your stuff, Sister, and next time you'll know better—in the end they did break down enough to tell me that from the Pocket of Pond-in-the-River there is an old hauling road

of the Thurston Brothers leading in the general direction
of C Pond. When I came to the end of that, at Thurston's
Number Four camp, I was on my own.

We started early in the morning, with sandwiches, compass, camera, and my yard-square, red bandana handkerchief without which I never stir a step off the premises. It's
the handiest rig I own. It can be used for a belt, a scarf, a
rain hat, a sling, a cage for small game, a reticule, canoe
caulking, a berry pail, a dog leash, a distress signal, or to tie
up a boat or gag a bandit. I've used it for all except the last,
and I still have hopes of that. We paddled the mile across
the Pond, which was dead calm and lovely, with wreaths of
steam curling over the surface, and landed in the green
watery shade of the Pocket. And sure enough, there was an
old pulp landing at the end of the grownup and ferny ves-
tiges of what was once a tractor road, leading, heaven be
praised, in the right direction. We hauled out the canoe,
hitched at our belts, and set out.

The footing was poor, but the woods were shadowy and
cool and we all felt fine. We referred to the compass off
and on and we were headed right. Lynn and I got into a discussion about the advisability of depending on moss growing on the north side of trees, for finding direction in the
woods, and agreed that that was so much baloney. There
was a chance it might work on a tree growing in the open;
but in deep woods, moisture and wind are about the same
all around, so moss-growth is where you find it. We stopped
to look at a few trees, found them evenly mossed, and con-
gratulated each other on our joint emancipation from folklore. In the meantime Virginia and Alice, who are respec-
tively editor and librarian, were having a session on writers
they had met and what they thought of them as persons.

I think the conclusion was that they are like anybody, only slightly less bright.

Then the trail forked and it was then I realized that while I was the native, the Maine guide, and the hostess rolled into one, I was up against some competition as a woodsman. I submit right now that a man who is supposed to be tied to a desk, reading manuscripts and being nice to authors, has no right to know as much about the woods as Lynn Carrick does. *I* was supposed to be in charge of the safari, so what business had he arguing me down on which branch of the fork we took? But he did, and, may the curse of the crows land on him square-footed, he was right; because within fifteen minutes we came out into a lumber-camp yard, which was exactly what we were supposed to do. That was where the hauling road ended, according to rumor, and that was where the hard part started.

The camp seemed deserted, although smoke hung over the cook-shack chimney. We stepped out of the shade into the clearing and realized for the first time, as the sun smote us, that it was a hell-hot day. Then the door of the blacksmith shop flew open, a man stepped out and shouted "Missus!" and came as near falling on my neck as respect for a married lady would permit. I looked at him, cried "Frank Burke!" and the klatsch was on.

For I have known Frank Burke for years. He's been a lumber-camp blacksmith all over this territory ever since I've lived here. One winter he smithed at Jim Barnett's camp a quarter of a mile above us on the river, and that winter he nursemaided Rufus, then three, more hours than I did. He'd let Rufus hold the horses' hooves during shoeing. Actually the hoof was in a leather sling, but Rufus thought he was helping, so that was all right. Once Frank and Ralph and I spent a whole day fussing over a blind horse that had walked off the edge of the ice into the channel down the middle of the Pond-in-the-River and was obviously on the verge of the horse version of pneumonia. We had him in the blacksmith shop where it was warm, and we ran miles around him, keeping him covered up with blankets. He recovered in time and made a very good twitch-horse, if you could keep him on open roads. He was gentle and clever, but since he couldn't see, in the woods he was useless, falling down, running into trees, and becoming more terrified by the minute, poor thing. Frank kept him for his own horse for the rest of the winter, since what timber he twitched into the shop for sleds and racks could be cut on the sides of the open Carry Road. One of the first things I asked Frank that C Pond morning was whatever became of that horse. But he didn't know.

He asked me in turn if I'd heard about Snowball. I had to think a minute. Then I asked, "Horse or one of the men?" That wasn't as silly as it sounds. The winter that Frank worked at Barnett's they had a white twitch-horse named Snowball. A twitch-horse, by the way, is a single horse that works with a single man on piecework, in a lumbering operation. The pulpwood has to be yarded—stacked in piles in various central locations called yards. Some of the trees are a long way from the yard, so after they are felled and limbed out, a horse twitches—or drags—them in. So he's a twitch-horse.

A twitch-horse is permanent in camp, while men float in and out as the spirit moves. Sometimes one horse, as was the case with Snowball, will have a dozen drivers in the course of a winter's work. Since you never know when he drifts in, how long a man is going to stay, whether one night or three months, it's much easier to identify him by the name of the horse he is using than to learn his proper name. We had a raft of Snowballs that winter, including three Frenchmen and one Negro; but it was none of these that Frank meant. It was one I couldn't place, because Frank's description consisted of a reiterated, "Sure you remember him. Chunky joker. Wore a black-and-white checked shirt." Half the woodsmen I know answer to that; but anyhow, what happened to this chunky joker was that he fell off an upstairs porch in Berlin into the canal and drowned.

There are two things about Frank Burke. One is that he is the only person I have ever heard use the verb "mock" in its biblical sense. Most people use it to mean imitate. When Frank says, "Oh, I mocked him!" he means "I derided him." I like that use. The other is that while he calls himself a blacksmith, he is really a metal craftsman. He should be making beautiful lacy iron gates or airy balcony rails instead of horseshoes and sled shoes. He has the hands of an artist, strong and square and spare. But his horseshoes are works of art, really, and like any good artist, he knows he's good. If you say of any other smith that he is not a bad workman, Frank says scornfully, "Him! He couldn't shoe a sheep!" That is the final condemnation. I always want to ask, "Who wants to?" but I've never quite dared.

Frank insisted that we stay to dinner, so we did, although it was nowhere near noon. But since there were very few men in camp and what there were, were working so far back that they had taken their lunches and wouldn't be in until night, dinner could be any time the cook was willing to get it on the table. The cook was good natured and started slicing ham and smashing eggs at once, while I set out to worm out of him and Frank just how we got to C Pond from there.

I ran up against a stone wall. They both admitted to having heard that there was a pond somewhere over yonder, but they both hastily disclaimed any personal or even secondhand knowledge of it. Although they had been in that camp for over a year, they'd never walked over to the pond and nobody they'd ever heard of had either. They wouldn't actually swear that there was a pond there. They made that very plain. If we wanted to go off on a wild-goose chase, all right; but never let it be said that they had encouraged us in our folly. Their only contribution was that if we followed a well-defined tote road out of the camp yard, we'd pass a sawmill, come to a bridge over a brook, turn left up a mountain, and come to another camp. Someone there might know something, maybe. But why didn't we just call it a day, eat our ham and eggs and tomatoes and pickles and bread and butter and pie and cake and cookies, and go on home where we belonged?

And face Ralph's and Gerrish's sneers? Not by a damnsight! We drank the rest of our coffee, said good-bye to our hosts, and set off down the tote road.

Boy, she was a scorcher! We went a mile through the worst slash I ever saw, so tinder-dry and hot that you wondered why the whole works didn't just burst into flame. For hundreds of acres about us there was not even shelter for rabbit, except the sear, brown tops of the slaughtered trees left lying in heaps and windrows. Dead stubs reached up toward the sky, stark and bitter and ugly. It was a place of desolation, terrible in its heat and hopelessness. We passed the sawmill, which was only a temporary affair powered by a tractor, and came out on a rough corduroy bridge over a cool, stony little brook that didn't show on our map. Lynn fished a folding cup out of his rear pocket, we drank a quart of brook water apiece, and consulted the compass. The road went, as advertised, to the left up a mountain, but according to our calculations, C Pond was slightly off to the right. To the right there was not even the suggestion of a trail. We held a council of war and decided to go up the mountain to the camp and ask for directions. By this time we were getting stubborn.

I'd really like to go over there again and take a look at that mountain. It can't possibly be as steep as I remember it. The Matterhorn isn't that steep. Nothing is that steep. We puffed and we panted and we sat down on rocks to rest—especially me. Lynn is a mountain climber from way back, Virginia is lean and long legged, and Alice is built on the general idea of a shetland pony, small and wiry; but I'm fairly well upholstered and more than fairly physically lazy. That mountain was my gethsemane. I was just about to holler "Uncle," when we saw, coming down the road, four men.

They were woodsmen I knew, even without considering the taken-down, steel-framed bucksaws they carried. You can't mistake a woodsman, once you know the breed. That they were leaving camp—the camp we were struggling toward, of course, since that was the only camp there was—was apparent in the fact that they had on clean shirts, even a white shirt in one case, and were carrying their turkeys—knapsacks to you. I said silently, "Praise the Lord!" and sat down on a stump.

They drew abreast of us, walking lightly and rhythmically, with their eyes on the ground. A woodsman never speaks first, because how does he know you care to be spoken to by a woodsman? He'll mind his own business and you are free to mind yours. As far as outward appearances went, we might have been nonexistent. So I said, "Hello. Hot day. You men quitting?" You get so you talk laconically in the woods.

Their eyes lifted and their teeth flashed in their bronzed faces as they halted. "She damn hot," the tallest one, the one in the white shirt, agreed. He spoke with a slight Finnish accent and he had the clean-scrubbed look that Finns somehow manage to achieve even in the woods. "Too hot to work in the cuttings. A man drop dead of the heat this morning, so we here think it's time to fly. Next it might be one of us."

I asked who dropped dead and he told me, but it was no one I knew, for a wonder. After over a decade of living in the lumbering country, I've what is known hereabouts as a "head-yanking" and "name-saying" acquaintance with scores of lumberjacks.

Lynn broached the subject of C Pond. Three faces were blank, but the Finn responded. "Is that her name? The pond with the high bluff at the east? I can show you. Last winter I walk over there one Sunday for the fun. There was no trail, so I spot her out. Come again to the bridge and I will put you on the spots." He looked regretful. "I didn't spot her good. It was for me alone. Nobody but me, I thought, goes to that pond."

It was wonderful to be walking downhill for a change. There is a school of thought that walking down a mountain is harder on the muscles than walking up it. Not for me, it isn't. I haul myself up a mountain. Gravity hauls me down. All I have to do is see that one foot is put ahead of the other, a purely automatic procedure. We came out onto the bridge again at a lively clip, and the Finn lay down his saw and swung his turkey off his shoulder.

"Wait for me here," he told his companions, and turned to us. "The spots do not start here. I must show you." He plunged into a tangle of undergrowth and dead tops which looked too thickly interwoven to allow the passage of a weasel. But when we came out on the other side, there was an old woods road leading to a pulpyard. We'd never have found it by ourselves. We left the pulpyard and cut uphill for a way, and there was the first spot, a clean gold slash on a pine. "She is not spotted good," the Finn repeated. "If I had known—but I think you follow her. Every hundred feet, maybe, I spot her, but if you lose the spots, remember—on the right keep the swamp, on the left keep the side of the mountain. You walk between mountain and swamp and you find the pond. If I had known," he apologized again, "I would have spot her good. But no one, ever, goes to that pond."

Alice looked at him. "You mean you're the only man in the whole country who could direct us to C Pond? If we hadn't happened to meet you, if we'd been fifteen minutes earlier or later—?"

"That is it," he said simply. "No one has the curiosity to know the country. It is a thing I do not understand." He bowed gravely and I'm afraid we were too overcome with our phenomenal luck to thank him properly as he left us.

Then Virginia did something for which I have always held her in high respect. She announced, "I guess I'll lie down and take a nap. You three can pick me up on the way back. I'll be down below in the pulpyard." That takes courage. If I'd been dying on my feet for sleep, I'd never have dared to do more than suggest a short breather. I'd have been afraid of public opinion, of disdainful stares down elevated noses, of critical comment. There is nothing so completely idiotic as not taking a nap when you feel like it, when there is nothing whatsoever at stake, but I wouldn't have had the guts to do it. Virginia did, more power to her! I watched in awed silence as she walked back down the slope.

Then we got busy. I took off my peerless bandana, which I'd been wearing at the ready, draped through my overall straps, and tied it to a sapling. That was to mark the point at which we would give up looking for spots on the return trip—should we live and prosper—and start downhill. Alice took up her belt a notch and stubbed out her cigarette on a mossy stone. Lynn started peering ahead for the next spot, and just as I was thinking, "Well, really now! If he imagines he's going to out-woodsman *me!*"—he found it on a birch. Alice gave me a satiric side glance.

I don't know what that Finn would have called a good job of spotting. His was good enough, even on a new, un-swamped, unused trail. Swamping is clearing out bushes and making a swath through the forest. A new trail is usually swamped and spotted, because it's easy to lose the way on one. After a few years the bushes grow back along the sides and the spots moss over, but then, if the trail has ever been in at all common use, it doesn't matter. Anyone at all woods-wise can follow an old trail. Even if no one has been over it for several years, even if there is no visible evidence of the passage of others, even if the spots are gone and the ground covered with fallen leaves, you can feel where people have walked. It's a sensation in the soles of the feet; or maybe it's psychic. I don't know.

The question didn't come up that day. What we were following wasn't a trail. Only one man had been over it, and he on snowshoes. His feet had never pressed the naked earth. We had his word that this was the direction, and we had his spots to follow. We could trust him or not, as we chose; and somehow he had inspired trust. We cruised along like a trio of hounds, looking for his slashes bright on the trunks of trees and always finding them. He was a good woodsman, that Finn. We never knew his name. We didn't know his past or what became of him after he said good-bye to us. His life touched ours for ten minutes, and in that time we knew him for what he was, a man courteous, curious in the best sense, and kind. I'll love that Finn to my dying day.

Before we expected it we saw the glint of open water through the trees, and we knew we were at C Pond, although we didn't believe it. We'd acquired a certain Holy Grail attitude. We were seeking the nonexistent, the ideal, and in the search lay the reward. We were having fun looping through the woods. Actually finding the pond was so much frosting on the cake. We thrashed through a final hemlock blowdown and stood on the shore of a placid, reedy, deserted little body of water. We were there, believe it or not.

The first thing we did was to take off our shoes and socks, roll up our pants, and step into the water. Nobody suggested it. We just did it. The mud oozed up between our toes and the knife-edged reeds sliced our shins. We didn't care. We were at C Pond. We ambled along the shore, knee deep in warm water, pointing out to each other the features of the place. At the east end were the bluffs, spruce-crowned faces of stone rising high and abrupt against the sky. They are impressive and wild and lovely. We wished aloud, singly and in concert, that we had time to climb them, and in the next breath we started planning an overnight trip to the pond. We'd come by canoe up the Dead Cambridge, if there were enough water in it to float a canoe and if there weren't we'd come anyhow and drag the damn thing. We'd bring blankets and food for a day. For two days. We might as well really go all out for this, once we were at it. We'd climb the bluffs and swim and fish and loaf and have a time for ourselves. We picked out a camp site, discarding a fallen-in trappers' shack on the far shore and choosing a little beach backed by a grassy clearing which must once have been a pulp landing. It was a good expedition, even if we haven't got around yet to taking it. We will one of these days.

Lynn took some pictures, just to prove in case we encountered skepticism that we'd made our objective, and we waded back to our starting point. We discovered that we'd picked up a few bloodsuckers, but even that didn't dampen our enthusiasm for C Pond, each other, and our combined intrepidity. We pulled them off, dressed our feet, and started back along the Finn's spots. The red handkerchief was right where we expected it to be—a phenomenon not as natural as it sounds. Things are always where you left them in the woods, of course, but even a good woodsman can get what is usually termed a "mite turned 'round." That's not the same as being lost, you understand, although I have never yet been able to pin anyone down to where the one stops and the other starts. I know a man who was a mite turned 'round for three days before he got himself straightened out enough to get home, but he insists he was not lost. He should know. It happened to him. I retrieved my bandana and we cut down the slope. Virginia was right where we expected her to be, too; and after we'd plowed through the God-awful whinnigan—a whinnigan is a tangle of tops and blowdown and the noun is *always* preceded by the adjective "God-awful" —so was the bridge. And coming down the side of the mountain, bouncing over the rough tote road, was a four-horse tote team.

Our thumbs all went up in the hitch-hikers gesture, and the driver reined in his horses. "Hi, Mis' Rich. Long way from home, ain't you?"

I looked at him again. "Claude Ferrin!" Claude used to be a feeder for Jim Barnett and I've known him for years. "Who you working for now?"

He spat over the wheel. "Wade Thurston, up the mountain. Where you bound?"

"Pondy River," I told him, using the woodsmen's name for Pond-in-the-River, considered effete around here, and he said he'd lift us to Number Four.

I knew what he meant, of course: Thurston's Number Four camp, where we'd had lunch. That was easy for me now. But before I went completely native, I used to be baffled by such designations. We'd be traveling with a guide through country new to us, and stop to ask directions. This is what we'd get: "Keep the trail up to Thirteen and then veer off west for a couple of twitches till you come to an old tote road. That'll take you into Seven and you just go downstream from there." The guide always seemed to follow the thread, but I never did, especially after we'd arrived at Thirteen or Seven and found there nothing at all except raspberry bushes and scrub fir.

Now I understand. Seven and Thirteen were once the sites of lumber camps. On a large operation the camps are numbered instead of named. After the operation is over and the camp torn down and the clearing grown up again, the point on the map where once it stood is still called One or Thirteen or whatever. If two jobbers are operating in the same general territory, the number may be qualified, as Thurston's Four to distinguish it from Barnett's Four.

But it's still just a spot in the woods. In a country where there are very few landmarks, any means of identifying a point is a real convenience. The couple of twitches? Oh, a twitch is the distance an average twitch-horse can haul a tree without resting. It's the woods' equivalent of a city block.

We climbed aboard and Claude and I started swapping gossip. "Saw a friend of yours last week," he said. "Wes Farris. Wanted to be remembered to you, case I saw you ever."

I should certainly hope so! Wes Farris is one of my favorite people in all the world. I don't know how old he is. He's looked exactly the same for all the decade I've known him. Some people say he's well over seventy and some say he's well on to eighty. Either could be right. "What's Wes doing now?" I asked, because I really wanted to know.

"When I saw him he was standing in front of the store in Errol stopping cars. Didn't make no difference who they were, Errol cars, Berlin cars, Out-of-Staters, he stopped them all. He was giving away beer."

"He was doing what?" I was startled.

"Giving away beer. Had a couple of cases on the road beside him and he give a bottle to every person in every car. No reason. Just feeling good."

Well, come to think of it, I wasn't surprised. I'd heard before about Wes when he was feeling good. I'd heard about the time he came off the drive, chicken-hungry. He hadn't had any chicken since the ice went out, and he wanted some. He wanted a lot. He arranged with an Errol woman to cook some for him, if he'd get hold of some, and he primed himself for the search with a black bottle. The more he sampled his bottle, the chicken-hungrier he got. He finally reached the conclusion that the sensible thing for him to do was to go out into the country, find a farm with a lot of chickens, and buy all he thought he could eat. Just as he was mulling over the problem of transportation, he saw the school bus parked for the week end, in a field. So he borrowed that.

He managed to acquire twenty-four chickens, which he turned loose in the back of the bus, and went back to Errol. He wanted them all cooked, and while the cooking went on, to pass the time he finished his bottle. The woman who was doing the cooking decided that two-three were all he'd eat, so that's all she cooked; and as it happened she was quite right. The rest of the chickens were left in the bus until Monday morning, when they were discovered by the bus driver. I've heard that the bus driver was not entirely pleased. Twenty-odd live chickens can make quite a mess over a week end.

Wes is a man who lives by his principles. One fall the Brown Company put a crew into Pond-in-the-River wangan to rebuild their towboat, the *Alligator*. Wes was on the crew. It was late in the season and the men were becoming nervous about getting caught in the freeze-up, so the boss asked them if they'd care to work on Sundays. The consensus was that they would.

I went up to the wangan one Sunday morning and found them all as busy as bird dogs. The cook was cooking and the cookee was peeling potatoes. Half the crew was caulking seams and the other half was driving spikes and planing planks like mad. There was definitely an air of urgency about the whole place, until I went into the barroom. Just to keep the record straight, the barroom has nothing whatsoever to do with alcohol. It's just the bunkhouse. On a bunk lay Wes, idly turning the pages of an ancient and tattered *True Story Magazine.*

"You sick, Wes?" I asked in some alarm.

"Nope." He turned another page, viewed with distaste the picture of a lush blonde fighting off a smooth, mustached number, and slapped the magazine shut. "Ain't no one can make me work Sunday. It ain't Constitutional. A man has a right to a day a week off for himself. Let them other jokers work if they want to, more fools they. I don't work Sundays." He rolled over on his face. "But by Jesus, Missus, ain't I going to be glad when it comes to-morrow morning and I can get back on the job."

I once heard Wes refuse to accept ten dollars that another river driver claimed he owed to him. "I don't rec'lect you owing me money," he said.

" 'Course you don't, you Jeesley fool. You was drunk when you lent it to me. You didn't know nothin'. Here, take it."

Wes folded his hands over his knee. "I don't take no money I don't rec'lect nothin' about lending," he said with dignity; and he didn't.

I love Wes Farris. He told me once that kindness was more important than cleverness, since there are a lot of clever people kicking about, but very few kind ones. He told me once that there are two kinds of people in the world, good and bad. The joker in the deck is that the good decide which is which; and ain't he right!

We climbed off the wagon at the entrance to Number Four, considerably shaken. If you've never ridden on a springless tote team over an ungraded tote road, you don't know what I'm talking about and I can't explain. If you have, you do, and no explanation is necessary. We said good-bye to Claude and struck off toward Pond-in-the-River.

We were all what my mother calls "above ourselves." She means intoxicated with the heady brew of success. We were silly and cocky, and don't ask me why. There's nothing very remarkable about what we'd done—just set out to find a pond and then found it. We knew that, but it didn't make any difference. We felt simply swell, invincible and superior. We tramped along, talking and splitting our sides at each others' witticisms. I don't remember one of the priceless gems of humor we were bandying back and forth, and I suspect they were all pretty flat. We thought they were funny, and that's what counts. We came out into the Pocket, shady no longer but flooded with level gold rays from the western sky. A water bird flew up from our feet into the low sun, and we could see as under X-ray the structure of its body, as delicately intricate and marvelous as the anatomy of happiness, a thing of fire and fiber, bone and blood, full of the promise of the ecstasy of flight. I tell you, we felt *good*.

We came home just as supper was cooking. Gerrish met us first with the comment, "Thought 'twas time you'd ought to get your sports out of the woods, Louise. Most nightfall." But he couldn't make me feel bad.

Catherine announced that all we were having for supper was buckwheat cakes and maple syrup, because she'd done the washing that day. And that didn't make anyone feel bad. She ended by cooking one hundred and seventeen of them and they were wonderful.

While we were eating them, we told all about our trip to C Pond, all the miraculous coincidences, all the people we'd seen and the news we'd collected, everything. When we'd finished, Ralph said drily, "Well, it certainly sounds as though this has been 'Louise Rich Day.'"

And that's how we've all referred back to it always, although it was exactly as much "Lynn and Virginia and Alice Day" as it was mine.

CHAPTER VIII

The Crazy Spring

At the time of Ralph's death it was necessary for me to leave Forest Lodge on very short notice. I have raved and torn so much and so often about the foolishness of anyone's living sole alone in this country—liable as he would be to any one of a number of catastrophes, from breaking a leg or double pneumonia to burning the roof down over his head—that I wouldn't have had the face to attempt it myself, even if I had had the heart for it. Besides, I wanted to be with the children. So I just emptied the water pails and the teakettle, threw what food there was in the house out on the ground for the birds, piled the canned goods into a couple of crates to be left in the Parsons' freeze-proof cellar, closed the doors of the place, and left.

That's not the way to close a camp. A camp should be left clean, with the floors washed, the mattresses turned back over the foots of the beds and the blankets and pillows stored in chests or hung over lines to discourage mice. All matches should be put away in tight tin cans—I did do that—and all dishes not in cupboards should be turned face down. Food which freezing will not hurt—such as coffee, sugar, cereal, and split peas—should be stored in tight, metal containers. Mousetraps should be set at strategic points and the fireplace screens should be left in place so chimney swallows won't get into the house and die messily. Clothes and dish towels and linen should be packed away in drawers and boxes, lamps should be left ready to use, with paper bags upended over the chimneys to keep them free of dust, and the kerosene can and the kindling and wood boxes should be full. The place should, in short, be as nearly ready to move into as possible. When you open a camp there is enough to do without having to rustle the makings of a fire, fill and trim lamps, and wash dishes. Forest Lodge was not left in that condition, by any manner of means.

That was not the worst. It was the conditions outside in the yard that bothered me as spring drew on and I, in Andover, began to think of the ice going out soon, up on the lakes. The place was littered with tools, which I couldn't have picked up and locked away if my life depended upon it. I had had only five hours in which to work, and I was so stunned I couldn't think what to do about anything. The ground was covered with eight inches of snow, and most of the tools were under it, not where I had left them, but where Ralph had been working last. I couldn't have found half of them in a week. It didn't make any difference during the winter months that the doors of the house were all unlocked and a lot of valuable equipment was strewn around the place. There was nobody in the whole territory except the Parsons and the Millers, and they knew that if I had anything they wanted to borrow, they were welcome to go down and get it, and I knew that they'd return it punctiliously. But as soon as the ice was out, the spring log drive would start, with river drivers swarming all over the place, and the spring fishermen would be coming in. I don't want to impugn the honesty of either of these groups, but never·

theless it is true that if a woodsman sees a good ax or cant dog lying around unloved and apparently unwanted, he is apt to take it under his wing; and if a fisherman finds a camp standing open and deserted, he is impelled by curiosity to enter and inspect it. During the inspection—I really hate saying this, but it is true—some small article like a compass or a good reel is apt to sneak its way into his pocket. I have never been able to understand why well-brought-up people, who wouldn't dream of entering the house of a stranger in the city, feel free to roam at will through one in the woods. The foregoing isn't true of all woodsmen and fishermen, or even of most of them; but it's true of enough so that I thought I'd better do something about going home to the lakes before the breakup, so I could stand guard over my property.

So I spoke to Larry Parsons one day when he was Out on the semi-weekly mail trek, and asked him to let me know the last minute it would be possible for me to get up the lakes in the snow boat, since I didn't want to walk around the shore carrying clothes, typewriter, reference books, food for a month, and other assorted collateral on my back. A couple of weeks later he announced that next Tuesday would be the day, and by next Tuesday, Catherine and I, having persuaded her sister Eva to move in and take care of our miscellaneous young in our absence, were ready to go when Larry called. We had more junk than you could shake a stick at, including a bunch of red carnations that I'd decided to take to Al Parsons, since I knew from long woods experience that after a winter in the wilds, fresh cut flowers are individual miracles, things you remember from the dim past, but never expect to see again. At the last minute, Kyak jumped into the station wagon and refused to get out, so we decided to let him go, too. After all, while neither of us had the slightest fear of being alone in the woods, two miles from the nearest neighbor, there are times when you like to be warned of approaching invaders, and Kyak, although not good for much else, usually would bark at strangers. Thus caparisoned, we set out.

I suppose the same thing is true of anyone returning from exile to the land of his heart, to the stones that speak to him with meaning, to the roads that lead to known destinations, significant with the past, to the people who talk the same language, laugh at the same jokes, understand the same oblique allusions. You get a feeling like no other feeling on earth, but what it is I cannot put down on paper. It isn't excitement, although excitement is there. It isn't happiness, which is too small a word to encompass what goes on in heart and mind. It isn't contentment, because contentment is a passive emotion. Perhaps it's a combination of all three with something else, for which there is no word, thrown in for good measure. I don't know. I can't tell you; but if you've ever been there you know what I mean. You could cry or fly or die—you wouldn't be surprised to find angels walking tall beside you—you're on your way back home. That's how I felt when we crossed the bridge just outside Andover, swung up the little hill, and turned sharp left into the fourteen-mile climb to South Arm and the lakes.

It was almost spring in Andover. There were patches of bare ground on the Common and a big puddle of slush and water in front of the store. The roads were bare and muddy and people went around with their coats open in the middle of the day. But as we climbed, winter attacked us again from its last desperate stand in the mountains. The snow grew deeper and the black trees on the forbidding road-cramping cliffs were stiff and stark with cold. By the time we had reached the Arm we were back in February, the bitterest month of the year. The thermometer on the garage read four above zero, and a howling gale swept from the north down the empty length of icebound lake. Never was there a scene so desolate. The mountains stood black between the steel gray of the lake ice and the slate gray of the sky, and great ghosts of driven snow moved in parade before them. The little snow boat—a contraption with skis in place of front wheels and a tread-driven rear—huddled on the ice at the foot of the bank, looking lost and forlorn; but that was the only sign of the presence of man. All else was frozen waste. It was terrible in its loneliness—and it was, to me, beautiful beyond expression.

The first thing to do was transfer our load from the station wagon to the snow boat, and this involved countless trips between the end of the road and the edge of the ice through a hip-deep drift of snow. Kyak was no help. He, too, was glad to get back into God's country, and he was anxious for us to stop horsing around with typewriters and sacks of potatoes and cases of canned milk, and get going. So he galloped up and down the bank in front of us, taking care to be always right where someone would fall over him and dump a box of clothes into the snow. I parked my carnations on the front seat of the snow boat, where they would be safe, I thought. I thought wrong. A gust of wind, more furious than any before, snatched them and started for Florida with them. I howled in anguish, dropped the mail sack which I was carrying, and set out in pursuit. I overtook them after three hundred yards. The three-hundred-yard dash on drift-covered ice would tax a Nurmi, and my trackwork never was what you might call outstanding. I came back puffing and panting to find the load all transferred, the station wagon safely garaged, and Larry chopping out the waterhole in the ice so he could fill the snow-boat radiator. I called Al up, on the woods line, to tell her we were starting, and climbed into the back of the snow boat—which looks like a paddy wagon—with the freight and Kyak. Catherine had never been up the lakes in the winter and I bigheartedly let her ride in front with Larry, so she could see what went on. The carnations I buttoned to my bosom inside my sheepskin. I'd been through enough for them already. I wasn't going to have all that effort wasted by letting them freeze stiff before I could deliver them to my hostess.

That was a ride. It was as cold as the outer circle of space. It was rough. From the shore a frozen lake looks flat, but once you get out onto it, you find that that is mere illusion. It's as hillocky as a plowed field. Shut up in the back of the rig, I couldn't see a darn thing, and I felt like a kernel of corn in a popper. I was pitched and tossed from side to side and from floor to ceiling. I finally found that by sitting on one side, on the floor, and bracing my feet against the other, I could at least keep rightside up. Kyak in the meantime, however, had been having his troubles with the law of gravity, and it made him nervous. He whined appealingly and came and sat in my lap, laying his head trustingly on my shoulder. That was all right, only the big oaf was squashing Al's carnations. An eighty-pound Siberian husky doesn't do a bunch of flowers any good by lying down on it. I spent the rest of the ride fighting him off, fighting off toppling cases of canned peas, and fighting vertigo. But we finally made Middle Dam, at just about sunset.

The place looked good, even in the cold twilight, with

the cabins that go with the hotel and the hotel itself closed and shuttered, even with the wind whipping the bare branches of the maple trees in front of the Parsons' house and setting into eerie motion the empty swing in the little grove. Even though the snow in the yard was churned and dirtied by the coming and going of the sleds during the past month of wood hauling, the place looked good. It looked good, even though for the first time in my life I came to it without the certain knowledge that Ralph would be waiting for me there in Al's house, with a casual, "Hi, Babe," on his lips, and a look in his eyes that belied his offhand words. If you love a place—or a person—you just love it, in spite of anything.

When I took the carnations out from under my coat, they had lost a certain pristine something they'd had when the florist picked them that morning, but they didn't look too motheaten and Al gave every evidence of being pleased with them. After we'd cut the stems and given them a couple of aspirin, they perked up a little; so that was one silly notion that turned out to be reasonably successful. We ate supper —deer meat steak, known to you, probably, as venison but never to a woodsman by any such effete designation—sat around and chewed the fat for an hour or so, and went to bed. Catherine and I had a big day ahead of us to-morrow. We had to move into Forest Lodge.

The next morning was lovely. The sun shone hot on the snow and the sky was cloudless. We didn't know it then, but it was the beginning of a phenomenal spring. Larry hitched up the horses, Prince and Chub, to a wood rack, and we piled everything we owned, plus a ton or two of stuff like batteries, battery chargers, canned goods, and the cat, Carter Glass, which had been parked at Parsons for the winter, on the sledge, and set out down the road. The snow was knee deep on the horses, and they plowed ahead through it, resting by common consent at intervals. The cat yowled in the breadbox which we use as a cat-carrier when necessary, and Kyak plunged behind through the snow, or jumped aboard to rest his legs and bark condolence at the vocal breadbox. I lay spread-eagled on the load, looking at the sky through the bare branches of the trees and listening with half an ear to what Larry and Catherine were saying up front on the seat. It wasn't anything very important, but their voices made a pleasant murmur. It was a nice ride, because of its very uneventfulness. By noon we were at the Lodge, unloaded, and ready to settle in. By night we had everything put away, a couple of beds made up, and the radio connected and working. We were home at last.

The next two weeks were perhaps the queerest two weeks I have ever spent in my life—two weeks lifted entirely out of time. It was only March, but every day the sun shone as hot as August. Mornings I wrote and Catherine cleaned and cooked. Afternoons we both cleaned camp, and took sun baths. We went down to the float from which we swim in summer, stripped, and lay surrounded by ice water and snowbanks, and baked. I got one of the worst sunburns I have ever had during those two weeks. Twice a week we went to Middle Dam for the mail and to gossip. The first time we went on snowshoes, but after that the snow wasted so fast we could go barefooted—which means in this country without snowshoes. We took sticks and irrigated the road, since the melting snow had made a river of it. I don't know how much good we did, making little channels out of the ruts so the water could run off into the woods; but ever since I was a child, I've loved to play in water, and it was just as much fun as it had always been to drain a puddle, deflect a current, make a miniature spillway. Now that I was grown up, I had to have the excuse that I was fixing the road; but the real reason I was doing it was just for fun. One day, after we had the camps pretty nearly cleaned, we had a bonfire—another hang-over from childhood. Of course our story to each other was that all this trash had to be disposed of, and the easiest way was to burn it; but we both knew better. At long last, with no parental supervision, we could have a really good bonfire. We called up Joe Mooney, the fire warden, and asked if it was all right, and when he said yes, we started a fire in the middle of the road, between two snowbanks. That was at two o'clock. At eight we were still at it. We burned everything we could lay hands on for which we saw no immediate use. And I might add that most of the stuff had been saved for years and years—by Ralph because he was a saver by nature, and by me because he made me save it—against some improbable emergency, and that we haven't yet had cause to regret the passing of so much as a single old piece of strap leather or the volume of *Who's Who* for 1936. Saving can be carried too far, and I consider it too far when every cranny of your house is so stuffed with old junk that you can't buy a new toothpick because you have no place to store it. It was a wonderful bonfire, and it's wonderful to have a clean closet or two around the joint.

The day after the bonfire I talked with Al Parsons on the telephone and she told me that, although it was a month early by ordinary standards for such a thing to happen, the ice was now definitely unsafe, and that unless something drastic, like a week of sub-zero weather, should occur, it would probably go out in April. I'd known it to go out once on the twenty-eighth of April, and we'd talked about it ever since. Usually it goes out around the tenth of May—which, as Al pointed out, is plenty early enough, if you have to get cabins cleaned and a hotel ready to open, with no help.

"No help?" I asked. I knew she usually had her cabin girls and a cook come In early to open the hotel.

"We can't get anyone In now. The only way to get In is to walk around the shore, and you know that's too much to ask of female help. Anyhow, we haven't got our help hired yet. It's hard to find, nowadays, with everyone in shipyards and defense plants, so——"

"Hey, look, Al," I said. "How about Katie and me coming up and helping? We haven't got anything else to do right now. If we came up for five or six days, we could get enough cabins cleaned to open on—and you could be doing other things——"

"Do you really mean it?" she asked, and I did; I thought it would be fun; I'd never worked at a hotel in my life.

We had an early supper and left the house at five o'clock. At that time, although the ground was still covered with snow even in the open, the thermometer outside the kitchen window stood at 100. This was the first week in April, remember, in Maine. We waded up the road, carrying a few clothes in packsacks, with our shirt sleeves rolled up and our sweaters tied around our waists. I recalled that two years ago that day I'd ridden up the lake with Larry in the snow boat, carrying my infant Dinah, and worrying every inch of the way lest she freeze in the nine-below-zero gale. It didn't seem possible—but then, weather never seems possible to me.

The next morning, Catherine and I started our cleaning

duties, on a cabin called The Bungalow, the third up on the north side of the hotel, and I began my education in hotel management. Up to that time, wherever I stayed at a hotel, I'd just stayed there. If the room wasn't clean or the soap was missing or there weren't enough blankets, I registered displeasure. If everything was in order, I took it simply as my due. I'm different, now that I've been on the other end of the business. I know now how easy it is to get a room all in order except for a missing glass, make a mental note to bring one along the next time I'm down that way, and then forget all about it. I know all about policing up a cabin, walking backward to the door, sweeping behind me so it will be immaculate for the coming guest, and then going back to check, only to find that the cabin boy has been in to fill the wood box and lay the fireplace fire—and leave a clutter of chips and mud tracks all over the living-room floor. It's damned annoying. I got so I counted blankets and hung curtains in my sleep. Larry and Al and Catherine all insist—I think I can tell when they're lying, and they weren't lying this time—that one night I went to bed and to sleep early and when Catherine retired to the other twin bed in Al's guestroom, I sat bolt upright and announced in a terrible tone, "You're not to come in here until you wipe your feet!" That's how seriously I took my new career. Believe me, Catherine and I were cabin-cleaning fools, and all summer long I found it impossible to enter one of those cabins for the purpose of calling on a friend without taking a surreptitious inventory of its condition. Only great restraint prevented me from running a finger along picture tops or looking under beds for dust rolls. I felt and still feel proprietary toward all nine cabins on the north side.

In the meantime the weather continued hot, and the date

for the opening of the hotel, originally set at May 1, was shoved ahead to April 25. Whit Roberts and Doc Stuart and Fred Newton, who always come in before the breakup to paint boats, repair cabins, and do other chores around the place, walked up over the rotten ice, dragging their clothes and tool chests on a toboggan. It was a terrible trip, they said, with the ice honeycombed to hell and slush to your boot tops most of the way. They came ashore near the float and dropped in their tracks, too exhausted to move for minutes. The telephone rang at odd times, and Al took calls from panting fishermen in such places as Massachusetts, where the apple trees were blooming and the daffodils had gone by, wanting to know when the ice was going out. They'd all be there the next day, was the story. "Not before the twenty-fifth," she'd say with a fine false assurance, keeping her fingers crossed and her eyes on the widening strip of open water up toward the Narrows. Then she'd run down to the cabin called Trails' End, where Catherine and I were vacuum-cleaning mattresses, and inform us, "Sorry, girls, but I've got another reservation for two. Let's see; we could put them in Birch Lodge, so I guess that's next on the list. I'll dig out the blankets and curtains that go in there."

And still the sun shone and the hot south wind blew and the ice grew blacker and blacker. Wide rifts of heavenly blue appeared between the floes, and it became possible to get around in a rowboat through the serpentine channels. The only thing was, you had to watch the direction of the breeze, because a shift would close the water behind you with floating ice, and you'd be stuck where you were. Larry and the three workmen went over onto Rifle Point where the big boat was hauled out and got it ready to put into the water. The telephone continued to ring, Catherine and I added cabin after cabin to our list, and Al reluctantly shoved opening day up to April 20. Larry went to Portland and hired help. Things were shaping up. It looked as if we'd be ready to open by the twentieth, with luck. I hope you notice that "we." That's how Catherine and I had come to feel about the place.

The ice went out on April 14—the earliest date of its going in the history of the lakes. The spring breakup on a lake is not spectacular. Everyone who has seen a movie of the ice going out of a river has a notion of gigantic floes and cakes grinding and crashing. It isn't like that on a lake. It just lies there, getting blacker and blacker and more and more porous. I think the ice acts as a burning glass under the rays of the sun, and the whole thirty-to-forty-inch thickness finally becomes just a sponge. If there is a good stiff shifting wind to chuck the mass back and forth from shore to shore, that speeds the breakup; but if there's not, nothing happens until one day you look and it's gone. That morning when you looked out, there was still ice there. At noon it seemed darker and, strange phenomenon, heat waves danced over it, blurring the mile-distant hills of the other shore. Then between the taking out of a rug to shake over the rail of Trails' End and the going back to get it, the ice disappears, disintegrating into millions of minute splinters. The lake is free; the ice is out.

I don't know what gets into fishermen. Probably just an uncontrollable itch to go fishing. Any dope knows that the fish haven't been hanging around under the ice, unable to contain their burning impatience to get caught. The fishing is no good for days after the lake is clear. The fish are half dead—cold and slow and logy and completely indifferent to the sporting life. It takes almost a week for them

to thaw out enough to sit up and take notice of their re-
sponsibilities toward guests of the State of Maine. The Out-
of-State fishermen might just as well, or better, stay home
for a while and tend to their knitting. But no. The minute
they hear the ice is out they cancel all engagements, kiss
their wives good-bye, and flock to their pet fishing camps.
Al and Catherine and I debated the possibility of keeping
it a secret that the ice was out of the Rangeleys for another
week or so, but Fate and the radio and the press and the
Maine Publicity Bureau were all against us. Just as we were
saying to each other, "Now, whoever answers the telephone
the next time it rings be sure and·say the ice won't be out
until the twentieth——" when a mellow voice came in over
the radio. "The ice is out of the following lakes in Maine:
Sebago, Thompson, the Rangeleys——" We looked at each
other and groaned. "Oh God," Al said, "Larry'll have to call
the chef and all to come in to-morrow—— We've got to get
the help's quarters ready—— Larry'll have to get the
plumbers in about those pipes on the north side—— I wonder what we can get for meat—— Larry'll have to go to the
ration board to-morrow—— Louise, did you check up on the
porch chair situation?—— Lord, the office has to be cleaned
—— Did anybody happen to see the paper with the safe combination written on it?—— Catherine, do you know anything
about where the top of the big coffee urn is——?"

The telephone rang and Al answered it. "Yes," she said.
"No. Not until the twentieth—— Yes, I understand, but
we aren't ready—— No, we couldn't possibly before the
twentieth—— Yes, I know but—— We-e-ll—possibly, but——
Oh, all right, if you'll—— All right, I'll have Larry meet
you. Good-bye!!" She turned to us. "We're opening the
nineteenth," she said in a voice of doom.

And we did open the nineteenth, in spite of hell and high water and the fact that the waitress who had been engaged couldn't come for a week because she was having an impacted wisdom tooth treated. Catherine took off her cabin girl slacks, put on a green uniform and apron, and went into the dining-room. I did a quick shift from scrub woman to chambermaid, and Al and Larry doubled in brass as practically everything else.

I don't imagine anyone who hasn't been through the mill knows what it means to get a hotel into running order, especially a hotel which depends on boats for its transportation, fishing for its popularity, wood stoves for its heat and cooking, and luck and a long-handled spoon for almost everything else. You have to get the guests' rooms ready. That we had done. You have to get the dining-room set up. Hotel dining-rooms always seemed to me to be places of permanence. The tables are there, ranged in precise rows, snowy with white linen and rich with silver and glass. You go in and sit down and someone comes and takes your order. Pretty soon food appears before you from some unimaginable source, and you eat it. The dishes are wafted away, and you saunter out, replete and happy, with never another thought for them. I'd never seen a hotel dining-room undressed, and it's something to see.

The tables were all bare and piled up on one side of the room, because that spring they had painted the dining-room floor. They go in rows down the length of the hall. That sounds simple enough, but it wasn't so simple when we came to do it. In the first place, they differ in size. Some are what we-in-the-know call six-seaters and some are four-seaters. You can't just chuck them in anywhere, because at Middle Dam the dining-room has supporting posts down the center and the tables have to fit in around them. Well, that could be done, with a little figuring, except that the floor of the building heaves with the frost and never was very level to start with. So some tables have two short legs, and some have one, and some have all alike. If you can get them into the right places, turned the right way, they'll set evenly and not wabble when anyone leans an elbow on them. Al, who has a truly remarkable memory for detail, could remember where they went. But during the course of a cold winter some of the bumps in the floor had heaved higher and some of the valleys had sunk lower. So we had to put cardboard props under a few legs, and in really serious cases get Fred Newton and his saw to perform delicate operations. We finally got them in place. Then they had to be set. That wasn't so bad, only it took time. Finally when it looked lovely, we sat down at one of the tables and tried to pretend we were guests, with the idea of getting the guest reaction. We all lighted cigarettes, and because by this time we were all tired and silly, we started a guestlike conversation.

"Then I tried a Silver Doctor," I said, "and on the second cast this big salmon grabbed it. Damnedest fish you ever saw—out of the water more than he was in it and——"

Al took up the tale, "I had him on twenty minutes. My God, he'd have gone to ten pounds easy. Maybe more. You never saw such a fish——"

"I'd sure like to have had him to take home to show the boys in the office," Catherine chimed in, and we all joined the chorus, "but my leader snapped and he got away."

We giggled in a feeble manner, stubbed out our cigarettes, and went out to put the kitchen in order.

I'd never in my life been in a hotel kitchen until that spring, and I found it a fascinating place. There is a range for the chef and a stove for the pastry cook and a charcoal burner to heat the steam table. There's a gas plate for waffles and griddle cakes and a gas urn for coffee, both fueled, in this remote section, by portable cylinders of gas. There are four sinks—the pastry cook's, the chef's helper's, the white-dish washer's, and the back-hall girl's. There's a big refrigerator that belongs to the chef and a little refrigerator that belongs to several other people, and heaven help you if you stick your nose into either one of them. Heaven double-help you if you put a dish back into the wrong dish closet, or take hot water out of the wrong faucet, or use a wrong dish towel, or throw the pigs' garbage into the refuse pail or the refuse into the pigs' garbage pail. Or wash the pastry cook's bread pans with water. Or drink a glass of milk out of the wrong can. Or leave the steam table lid open. Heaven help you, period, I found out later; but that wasn't until quite a lot of water had gone down through the sluices.

That wasn't, for example, until after I'd spent two days being plumber's helper. The plumbers came in from Rumford, as planned, to repair and connect the network of pipes that lead to the cabins, each of which has its own bathroom. Catherine by that time had been promoted to waitress, but I was still operating at the old stand, and I knew—who better?—what ailed each bathroom on the place. I started out to do no more than point to the taps that leaked, the taps that wouldn't work at all, and any other feature of the plumbing that seemed out of kilter. I ended by crawling under cabins with a hazel-eyed plumber named Gordon—I never did find out his last name—and holding matches, wrenches, pipe solder or anything else his errant fancy dictated. I learned a lot about elbow joints and shut-offs, but

I gave up on the day that he herded me into a bathroom, asked me to hold up the end of a bathtub while he tightened the connection, and then left me standing there lifting while he got out the makings, rolled and lighted a cigarette, and went out to find the proper wrench. I'm good natured, but enough was enough; and holding up the end of a bathtub for fifteen minutes, more or less, was more than enough. I resigned my commission as plumber's mate.

I liked cabin work. I really did. During the time I did it, there were only men in camp, and they all had the kind of clothes I adore—soft woolen shirts, pliant leather jackets, beautiful corduroys. It was positively a pleasure to go in after the party had gone fishing and pick up the garments strewn over the place. It was worth washing ashtrays, making beds, and sweeping out—work which actually I didn't mind, since I was doing it alone. I'd much rather work alone on any job, anyhow; you can think your own thoughts over and above the routine, and you can go your own pace. I was a good cabin girl, if I do say so as shouldn't, leaving my cabins neat and clean and getting through my work by noon. That last item is a point more important possibly than the first. No guest likes a chambermaid snooping about his cabin while he is trying to take a nap or promote a game of poker or relax with a good book and a bottle of beer.

During my free afternoons I tried to do some writing up in Al's own private house, but unfortunately for me—although possibly it was fortunate for American Letters—that didn't work. Al's house overlooks the whole hotel and yard, and by this time I'd become so involved in the inner life of the joint that a leaf couldn't fall without my wondering why. I'd try a tentative opening line, glance out the window, see Larry hurrying down to the pier with a box of tools under his arm, and immediately go into a dither about what boat had gone wrong and why. Was it the big boat? That would be bad, because the cows were expected In to-day. Or maybe it was the Chris-craft, which would be equally bad, come to think of it, because he was supposed to go to Upper Dam at four o'clock and get some guests. Well, maybe it was only one of the outboards, so I needn't worry. I'd type another line and look up to see Al dash out of the office, round the corner on two wheels, and disappear in the direction of the icehouse, laundry and storeroom. Now what ailed her? What had happened? Where was she going?—— You get the idea. So I resigned literature in favor of laundry, which Al was doing on a sort of catch-as-catch-can basis. In other words, she'd run through a washerful of clothes in odd ten minutes between answering the telephone, making out the menus, answering questions, hunting up spare blankets for the man who was cold last night, and finding a box of paprika for the chef. So I thought I might as well make myself useful there.

I liked the laundry work. Again, I was either working alone or with Al, with whom I always have a lot to talk about, since we have lived for nine years in the same bailiwick, among the same people. Then there was a certain amount of social life connected with the job. Any time the other help had nothing better to do, they'd drop in for a minute to exchange the time of day, sitting on the table by the mangle and swinging their legs. Catherine and Rose Howe—the other waitress—would tell us that Mr. Smith was a funny eater who didn't want anything for lunch except crackers and milk; and I'd volunteer that I should think he would be, judging from the number and variety of pills he had standing on his bathroom shelf. That was enough to make anyone eat funny. Or they'd say Mr. Jones was fresh, and Dr. Abbott was simply swell, and we'd all tear them to pieces. Believe me, next time I go to a resort to stay, I'm going to be careful. I never realized before how much the back hall knows about the front hall, nor how accurate their diagnoses can be. The back hall, by the way, can mean either the place where the help eat and work, or it can mean the help themselves. The front hall is the guests' dining-room, but not the guests. Guests are either guests or sports. Then Al would say to me that another basket of clothes was ready to hang out, and I'd grab it and run into the clothesyard, with a parting plea not to say anything important or interesting while I was gone.

I like hanging out clothes, if I have enough line space and plenty of clothespins. The hotel had both. I like to make myself a system—the sheets here, the pillowcases here, the towels here, and any odd garments over there— so that when we come to take them in, they're all sorted. I like to be out in the sun and wind, with the clean clothes flapping around me, and the lines filling up as tangible proof of something accomplished. I *love* to take in clothes, they smell so good. I never iron sheets for that reason. Maybe they look better all smoothed out and creased. Some sensitive souls say they feel better on a bed. But even if the roughness corrugated my skin, it would have to be corrugation to the bleeding point to make me give up the purely sensory pleasure of going to bed between sheets smelling of wind and sun and fresh air. It's seldom that a luxury can be obtained by the actual saving of work for oneself, but this is one time when it can, and I esteem it accordingly.

Ah, happy days as chambermaid and laundress, as they say in the type of old-fashioned novel that amuses me like anything in small doses, and irritates me to the screaming point in large. Too soon were they over. I wandered into the back hall one afternoon to find the chef's helper obviously coming down with something. She was miserable and looked it, but she was trying to keep on the job. She was a nice woman and I liked her, and we couldn't wash because it was raining, so I told her to go to bed and I'd do her work. This wasn't pure generosity. I had ulterior motives. I wanted to see how the back hall and kitchen functioned, and the best way I knew was to work there myself. A writer never knows when miscellaneous information will come in handy. I might need some time, for purposes of plot or background, some straight dope on backstairs life in a hotel. And believe me, sister, I got it.

The title, chef's helper, is extremely misleading. It sounds very grand and important, as if you stood about in tall cap and uniform, handing rare condiments to the chef, while he stirred and tasted delicate sauces. Actually it means that you peel the vegetables, wash up the chef's pots and pans, and scrub his section of the floor. You're the kitchen scullion, in short. At Middle Dam, you also make the salads, and that's all I did like about the job, except the fact that it was An Experience. I was a simply lousy chef's helper, as anyone who was working in the kitchen at the time will gladly testify. I ended by working there for a month, since the woman who had had the job really wasn't well enough to stand the gaff. She took over my cabins and I took over her vegetable knife and dishmop, while Al and Larry conducted a house-to-house search throughout the State of Maine for a suitable successor to me. During that time everyone was nice and patient with my shortcomings, but I was very definitely considered by the other kitchen help as the not-quite-bright little sister of the family.

In the first place, I didn't understand the rigid boundaries that separate one person's sphere of duties from another's. Take the matter of floor washing, for example. I was supposed to wash the floor around my own sink, the salad-room floor, and the floor in front of the chef's range and under the steam table. Mrs. Gonya, the white-dish washer—that means she washed the good dishes used in the guests' dining-room—was supposed to wash the floor around her sink and under the two tables where the waitresses did their silver and glasses and loaded their trays. Rosella, the pastry cook, did the floor in her corner, which was clearly bounded by her own serving-table. It was between Mrs. Gonya and me that the arguments arose—good-natured arguments, I'll grant you, but arguments all the same. I couldn't see that it made an awful lot of difference whether I washed one plank too many or too few, while she had it right down to the crack in the floor where her domain ended and mine began. After I'd been on the job a few days, cracks didn't matter, though. Her section of the floor was always white as a bone, while mine was coffee-colored just after I'd mopped it, and tar-colored the rest of the time. The line of demarcation was painfully clear.

But it was the vegetables that got me down. Did you ever sit down in front of a bushel of potatoes and know you had to get through it before ten o'clock? It's discouraging, especially if, when you are just getting into the swing of the thing, the chef starts hollering about where are those three large kettles? He needs them right away. You lay down your knife, fish the kettles out from under a pile of dirty pans, and scour them down. By that time the chef wants to know whether those potatoes are for lunch to-day or next Sunday's dinner, and don't forget the ten bunches of carrots to be scraped and sliced. And the salads. This noon we'll have green pepper and beet, so how about slivering up some peppers and cutting beets into fancy shapes. In vain do you plead for lettuce and tomato, which is quick and easy. We had that day before yesterday and he has a reputation to think of, even if you haven't. So you shove your sleeves a notch higher, push back your hair, and redouble your efforts. I *hated* those darn vegetables, and those persons whom I discovered not to eat potatoes won my personal popularity-poll hands down.

I did learn some things, though, from the chef in spite of the fact that my head was much more often deep in a potato basket, dishpan, or mop pail than it was bent over the range. I learned that if you haven't any parsley to chop for a garnish—parsley was off the market right then—you can chop celery tops fine and get by with it. I learned how to use a French knife—one of those wide-bladed, tapering, thin knives that chefs use as a third hand. The chef I worked under—Pat—could do anything with one. The method for fine chopping was as follows: Pile the material to be chopped in the middle of a chopping board, take the handle of the knife in your right hand, and hold the point down to the board with your left. One hand is on either side of the pile of celery leaves or potatoes or whatever, in the middle of the board. Then pump the blade up and down, moving from rear to front of the pile and back again, keeping the point always hinged on the board. When the pile is spread out too much, scrape it together again and keep on until it's as fine as you want it. This is a lot easier and quicker than a chopping bowl and chopper. I learned that to slice an end of ham very thin without cutting yourself, you put it face down on a board at the very edge of the table, place another board on top of it under pressure, and work with your knife between them.

I learned that any knife less than razor edged is an insult to a chef and that anyone who abuses the chef's knives, cutting with them on a metal surface or chucking them into the dishpan with the other cutlery, might just as well leave the country at once, if she values her life. I learned that you never throw away anything. The blossom ends of tomatoes and the outside stalks of celery and leaves of lettuce go into the stock kettle, which stands on the back of the stove. So do the half-cup of French dressing left in the bottle and the scraps of green pepper left over from the salads, and the ham bone that shows up when you clean the refrigerator. I learned how to treat a head of iceberg lettuce. I, in my simple ignorance, have always either sliced it off, for a shredded effect, or torn leaves from the outside toward the center. That's all wrong. You cut out the core with a knife and hold the head under the cold water faucet, so that the water will run hard into the resulting hole. At the same time you pull gently, placing your thumbs in the hole and your fingers around the head. The water works between the leaves, washing and separating them gradually, and you end with nice crisp clean pieces to the greater glory of your salads.

I learned the importance of food arrangement on the plate. Two gallons of mashed potatoes—incidentally, the chef doesn't love his helper if she leaves eyes in the potatoes on the day he's going to mash them, because they show up as black unappetizing specks—two gallons of mashed pota-

toes in a kettle aren't too glamorous a vision, nor is a huge
pan of broiled chops. They're a bit overpowering. But the
chef fusses and fiddles with them on the plates, even going
so far as to dump them back and start all over with a clean
plate when something goes wrong, and by the time the
girls have taken them into the dining-room, they look
wonderful. I thought at first Pat was being old-maidish
about the whole thing, standing back to view the effect of a
lemon slice and moving it an eighth of an inch to the left,
but I finally came to the conclusion that he was right. At
any rate, I haven't been able to eat in a restaurant since
without giving my dinner a quick once-over before I com-
mence eating it, and making a mental note of the number
of points I'd award for the garnish and the three I'd take
off for the drop of gravy over near the spinach.

You know, there's a lot to serving a meal in a hotel
kitchen. Up until about eleven o'clock, everything is very
easy and comfortable. The waitresses are buzzing around
in their old clothes, which they've changed into from uni-
forms right after breakfast, polishing glasses and cleaning
silver, and asking each other highly technical questions
like, "Does that trout in the fish box belong to your Hazen
party or to my Rogerses?"; or "Are you going to change your
tablecloths this morning?" The white-dish washer and the
back-hall girl are discussing their operations and returning dishes that somehow have wandered into each other's
sink. The chef is drinking another cup of coffee before
emptying the urn and trying to sing a harmonizing bass to
his helper's erratic version of "Bell-bottomed Trousers."
(I was the helper and I can't keep a tune.) The pastry cook
and one of the guides are fighting good-humoredly about

the fate of the two chocolate doughnuts left over from breakfast. Al comes in to take the chef's list of things he wants from the storeroom and stays to eat a warm cookie. Swene, who has been icing up the big refrigerator, drops a splinter of ice down my neck, laughs at my yowl, and tells me that's for putting a coffee can in the pigs' pail yesterday. It's fun.

But along around eleven o'clock the tension begins. The chef starts watching the clock and his braised beef. The waitresses say, "Now that's *my* tray and I don't want it touched; I just scoured the bottom of it," take a last look at their tables, and run along to change their clothes. I think, "Oh my God, I forgot to wash the coffee urn," and ask the pastry cook how many there are in the front hall, because I want to know how many salad plates to lay out. She doesn't answer me, because she's worrying about the meringue on her pudding and, anyhow, she'd like to know who took her pet spatula; if she ever finds out she'll—— The tension increases. I'm never going to get the salads out on time, and who hid the mayonnaise jar? I left it right here and nobody had any business moving it. The waitresses come back, all crisp and clean, with new faces on and their aprons tied back-side-to to save them from spotting. They start cutting their butter and getting their ice water ready, and asking each other with restrained courtesy to please not use the center tray-stand, because that's the one that goes with the six-seater, and you can't serve that big table from the end stands. The pastry cook announces under her breath that they'll just have to eat that pudding or go without; it's probably as good as they get at home, at that. The chef tells me to ring the back-hall bell. He's all ready to serve the help now, and then will I get him a dozen eggs out of the refrigerator and peel a mulligan full of onions? A mulligan is a Number Ten can, but I didn't know that, so I have to ask and he is very short with my benighted ignorance. I ring the bell and decide to skip lunch; my salads will never be done. The waitresses aren't done with their butter, either, so they keep on working. The back-hall girl comes in and tells us our lunch is getting cold, pauses a minute, and then informs me that that bowl I'm using belongs in her domain, and will I please return it. The clock moves around to twelve. It's time to ring the front-hall gong, so I say "All right to ring, Pat?" He says, "Oh, hold your horses. The guests aren't going anywhere," and tastes of his cream soup. Then he gives me a nod, and I go out and beat on the gong with a wooden mallet. Both waitresses run for the dining-room—they're supposed to be standing there when the guests enter—but one of them comes back and asks frantically, "Has anyone got a safety pin? My slip strap just broke."

The chef takes his place behind the steam table, the pastry cook starts laying out individual servings of the pudding and cutting pie, I count my salads and find I'm two short—someone stole a couple while my back was turned—and the white-dish washer announces that she hopes the girls will bring their dishes out promptly, because she has to wash her floor after lunch. I groan loudly. If she washes her floor, I'll have to wash mine. The chef gives me a dirty look and says, "Quiet! The guests are coming in now!" I'm quiet, properly rebuked.

Then the waitresses start coming out, and you'd never know them. They're full of business. Even their voices, which were normal and warm that morning, have changed. They're sharp and crisp and inhuman. "Four cream, two

tomato soup. Five braised beef and one plain omelet."
They take the appropriate dishes out of the steam table and
line them up on the shelf in front of the chef, where he can
reach them easily. All normal conversation stops. The chef
may say, "You didn't put your dishes up, Miss," or "Whose
order of turnip is that? Take it out of here." Or one of the
girls may say to another, "Hey, those are my two sliced
ham!" But that's all. The entire attention of everyone in
the kitchen is on getting food onto the front-hall tables,
hot and with quiet expedition. It's nerve racking for an hour
or so.

Then the peak is passed. Catherine comes in and says,
"I've got two more; how many have you got, Rose?" Rose
says only one, and I cheer silently. I'm coming out even
on salads after all. Rosella strolls over to Mrs. Gonya's sink
and asks, "Did they clean up on that pudding?" She looks
into the pigs' pail, sees no pudding and remarks, "Well,
I guess we got away with that." She grins at me. "You didn't
have any lunch. Want a piece of apple pie?" The chef says,
"Heck. Make yourself a hot beef sandwich first." Rose and
Catherine come in and say, "Whew! Everybody's out. Hey,
did you see me almost dump soup down Mr. Tarbell's neck?
Look, what do you do about serving your corner tables? I
can't get in behind mine. Chef, four people commented on
the beef. It was good. Anybody care if I have a cup of
coffee, and, Rosella, could I snag one of those hermits?
They look swell." The meal is over. We're all friends again.

But I'm glad I don't work in a hotel kitchen for keeps.
I couldn't stand three nervous breakdowns a day, day in
and day out. Whenever I eat in public now, no matter how
quiet and efficient the service or how appetizing the meal,
I picture to myself the silent inferno out back. I haven't

made up my mind yet whether this clairvoyance spices or ruins the meal.

Finally the Parsons found a man named Joe who wanted my job, and as far as I was concerned, he could certainly have it. I explained to him to the best of my limited knowledge what his duties were to be and that you cleaned the meat block with coarse salt and a wire brush twice a week, and gave him my blessing. And that was that. Al had found a laundress, everything else was under control, so I was out of work. I decided that the best thing for me to do was go home to Forest Lodge mornings, where I could write without the fascinating life of the hotel to distract me, eat my lunch there, and wander up to the hotel when I got around to it in the afternoon, picking violets and shagbush along the way for the girls to put on the dining-room tables.

This was a very practical thought, except that the minute I got back, I had to go down to the office and waste an hour or so of Al's time while she caught me up on the excursions and alarums of the morning. That's how I happened to become half-time office girl. As long as I was there, I might just as well answer the telephone, sell candy bars and post cards, issue fishing licenses, and hand out phony inside-tips to fishermen. It left Al free for more important things and gave me something to do. Compared with my stretch at being chef's helper, it was the life of Riley. One of the guides came in one afternoon and remarked, "Gee, Louise, to work up from chambermaid to office manager in two months shows brains. But I'm telling you, if you let yourself go any higher, it'll show an awful lack of them." And from what I have seen of the headaches of hotel ownership, I would say he was right-times-two.

Then one day I looked at the calendar and it was the

second of June. Good Lord, the kids would be coming home from school at the end of the week! Catherine and I had to go home and get ready for them. So we resigned and took the old Ford down the road one rainy evening. The Crazy Spring was over.

CHAPTER IX

The Dark Months

LIVING THE simple life is a very complicated matter, and one of the major complications is the educating of the young in a country where there are no schools, but where the authorities still hold a narrow view against a state of natural innocence so pure as not to include at least a nodding acquaintance with the tool subjects. There was a time not so long ago when people like us, who live far off the beaten path, could apply to the State to furnish them with a teacher. She would come and live with them and do what amounted to private tutoring, the State of Maine paying her wages and the family with whom she lived furnishing her board. But this policy has been abandoned on the grounds that an important part of education is learning to become a social creature, to participate in group activities, and to get along with other people. This is particularly necessary, so the State holds, for the adjustment of children who have lived in such isolated communities as ours. They have never had a chance to rub elbows with their peers, and the sooner they are exposed to the joys and sorrows of communal living the better for them. I have seen children who were educated under the old system, and the State is right. It is almost impossible for them to take their proper places in society when at last they do go Outside to school. They are as wild and shy as intelligent little animals. They don't know how to talk as the others talk, or dress as the others dress. They find the "civilized" points of view impossible to understand. As a result—the youth pack being completely heartless and barbaric—these children are made the butts of ridicule, and live, unhappy little pariahs, in what must be hell.

However, the fact that I see eye to eye with the State on this subject does not simplify my own problem. So every August I go through the same routine of looking for a furnished house on the Outside in which to park my children through the ten dark, or educational, months of the year. I've had three years of it so far, and lived in three different towns, all within a reasonable distance of Middle Dam. Since Dinah is only four, it looks as though I had a long stretch ahead of me.

The first year was in some ways the best and in some ways the worst. Ralph was alive then, so he and I lived in the woods and left Catherine on the Outside with the children, making only week-end and vacation descents upon them. That was good. One of the things that made it bad was that I had to sell Ralph the idea that it would be better for Rufus to have his own home to return to, from school, than to board in someone else's home where, no matter how good they might be to him, he'd still be a stranger in a strange land. At the time, when my sales promotion was in progress, we were entertaining fourteen guests at Pine Point and the only private corner in the whole joint, where we could have a good old family argument without an audience, was the bathroom. So every time he went in there to shower or shave, I slithered in right behind him, quick-like-a-cat, and delivered whatever new points I'd thought up since our last session. The hours I've spent sitting on the edge of the tub saying, "But look, Ralph, can't you see——?" or "Oh, for heaven's sake! Don't be so hidebound!" I finally wore him down to consent, if not to enthusiasm, and he said, "Oh, all right! But I'm too busy around here to go thrashing over the county, looking for a house. This is your idea. You can handle it yourself."

So all right, I thought; I will; and I called up Joe Mooney and asked him who was living in Jim Barnett's house in Upton. That would be a good house for us, if no one else was living in it and I could get hold of Jim and Jim would rent it. It turned out then that Jim had a logging job in the Thirteen Mile Woods somewhere and wasn't on the telephone. I asked Joe to leave word at the store in Upton for Jim to call me the next time he was in town, and to make assurance doubly sure, I wrote him a letter. That ought to take care of that, I thought. But the store forgot to give Jim the message and he never gets around to answering letters. In the meantime the opening date of school was drawing closer and closer and still I had no house. Finally I called Alice Hinckley in Upton and asked her to flag Jim sometime when he was going past and ask him if he'd rent his house to us. I'd forgotten she was on the school board, or if I remembered it, didn't appreciate the dire implications.

"Sure," she said. "I'll see Jim. But if I get the house for you, I'll expect you to board my teacher. The people she lived with last year have left town."

"Oh, *Alice!*" I said, "I don't *want* a boarder."

"You want a house, don't you?"

This was blackmail, but there didn't seem to be anything I could do about it, so I meekly said, "Yes."

She got us the house.

We moved the Sunday before Labor Day, Catherine and the three children and the high chair and the crib and boxes of sheets and bales of clothes and bundles of skis and snowshoes and sleds. I went along for two or three days to get them settled and Ralph abandoned his isolationist attitude sufficiently to run us down Umbagog as far as Davis Landing, which is the jumping-on place for Upton. It's really only a tumbled-down dock near a deserted sawmill that used to be run by a man named Davis, but it's a place to tie up a boat and it's near the main road. Cedric Judkin met us with his potato truck, we dumped the collateral aboard, I climbed onto the tailboard to guard the load, and we set off up the long lift of Hampshire Hill toward the town. The lake fell below us and spread out as we climbed, looking as lovely as it always does. I could see the *Puss,* a white speck on the blue, beating her slow and steady way north through the narrows near Jessie Potter's farm, and I divided my attention between watching it, seeing that none of our possessions fell off the truck, and returning snootily the stares of Out-of-State, Labor Day week-end motorists, all dressed up in their best hats, who quite obviously considered that they were being treated to a good example of quaint underprivileged backwoods Maine at its worst.

We liked the house at once. It is in the center of the town, a few hundred feet from the store, even nearer the school, and next door to the church. Across the street is an empty hotel and there's a huge barn on the uphill side of the house. This made it convenient, as Catherine pointed out. We'd have no neighbors peering into our windows. Conditioned as we were to living in the woods where we not only didn't pull down shades, but didn't even have them, this was providential. We were too old dogs at undressing in front of uncurtained windows to start learning new tricks at that late date. We set up Dinah's crib, put clothes away in bureau drawers, stowed the groceries in the cupboards, and made up the best front room for the teacher, who was due on the morrow-noon stage. Then we considered that we were at home and sat down for a quiet evening of reading and listening to the radio.

At nine the lights went out. This we hadn't bargained for. We debated whether it was curfew or trouble, changed the fuses without result, peered out of windows and failed to discover one gleam of light anywhere in the miles and miles of territory spread out under us, and decided we might as well go to bed anyhow. We were tired and pleased with ourselves and the world, a happy state in which to retire.

I undressed in the dark in the unfamiliar room I was to share with Rufus for the two nights I'd be in town, moving quietly and listening to the deep contented breathing of sleeping childhood with something like contentment in my own heart. I pulled back the covers gently so not to waken him, and just then the lights came on again. I stared, gasped, and squeaked in a voice I didn't know for my own, "Katie! Come here! Are these *bedbugs*?"

She crossed the hall in one bound, looked and nodded. They were. "What'll we *do*?" we asked each other.

I think Jim is going to cut my throat when he finds out I ever told anyone about this, so I'd better insure that he uses a good sharp knife and makes as painless a process as possible out of it, by saying right now that the rest of the house was entirely free of the things, and that he was entirely unaware of the condition of that bed when he rented the place to us. As a lumberman running several woods operations, he was obliged from time to time to put up for the night woodsmen on their way into or out of the woods. Try as they will, lumberjacks cannot keep free of lice and bedbugs all the time, and the last man who had slept in that bed had apparently been well populated. Fortunately the population had not had time to spread beyond the limits of that bed—but we didn't know that during that first moment of wild and awful surmise.

You know, you can do a lot of things when you have to, even in the middle of the night after a long day. First we snaked my poor child out of bed so fast he smoked, pitched his pajamas out the window, and gave him a bath to end all baths. Then we laid him away on the living-room couch while we tore every bed in the house to pieces with vigor and went over it with a fine-toothed comb. At two in the morning we decided that things were not as bad as they seemed. The rest of the house was all right. We could retire with easy minds. Rufus and I appropriated the bed we'd set aside as sacred to the teacher, and I tried to go to sleep. He'd never really waked up through it all.

That was an awful night. I'd tell myself, "Now you *know* nothing is biting you. You went over this bed yourself. Stop being silly and go to sleep." But something was, just the same. So I'd turn the light on and look. But nothing really was. I'd turn the light off and try to think about something else. I said all the poetry I know to myself, usually a sure-fire soporific. "The sea that bares its bosom to the moon; the winds that will be howling at all hours," I'd mumble, and sit up and turn the light on. No, nothing was crawling across my chest, so I'd turn the light off and recite doggedly, "They say the men here plow the snow. They cannot mean to plant it, though, unless in bitterness to mock——" There *was* something biting my elbow! On with the light! I had that light on and off four hundred and twenty-seven times before dawn bleached the windows, and every time I was mistaken. As soon as I could see my hand in front of my face I got up and dressed, met Catherine—who had had the same kind of night—in the hall, and we went down together and made ourselves some coffee. We needed bracing for the day.

At seven, Jim came in with the cheery announcement that he'd clean the cellar, he guessed, for us girls. (Girls by courtesy only; but Jim is a courteous man.) "Oh, no, you won't," we informed him. "You'll come right upstairs with us!" It would have been obvious from our tone to the most self-opinionated Lothario that we weren't being coy, so he came along. I never saw anyone so embarrassed in my life. We felt sorry for him, in spite of the night we'd just endured. He abandoned all cellar-cleaning dreams, gave us a gallon of gasoline and two paint brushes, and set out for Bethel in search of fumigating candles. "And hurry back," Catherine told him. "We want to get this mess cleaned up before the teacher gets here."

If you've never battled bedbugs—and I hope you never have; once was plenty for me—I can't possibly convey to you what we went through. It seems that they are crafty little devils, given to hiding in cracks in the furniture or down the mopboard, or in any small space. If you miss *one,* it always turns out to have been a female already pregnant, so you're right back where you started, a week or so later. We threw the mattress out of the window and dragged it around back of the barn, keeping a Sister Anne watch against passers-by who might deduce the cause of this action. Then we washed the whole room—and I mean the whole room, including cracks in the backs of bureau drawers and the coils of the radiator—with gasoline. We took the bed completely down, washed the joints, and put it back up. The place reeked with fumes and so did we. By the time it was aired, Jim was back with his sulphur candles, and we lighted them, sealing the windows and finally the door behind us with adhesive tape. Then we drew a long breath, just as the doorbell rang.

"That'll be the teacher," I said. "We're just in time." I fixed my face in a welcoming smile, went down and opened the door, and was confronted by two women. "Good morning," I caroled cordially. "Which one of you is going to live with us?"

They gave me the look one reserves for idiots. "Why— both of us," they told me.

My cordiality evaporated in nothing flat. "*Both* of you! Why, Mrs. Hinckley said—— Why, we aren't ready for two—— Why—— Step in and I'll call her up."

It didn't do any good. There really wasn't any other place for a teacher to live, so we ended by having them both, although we had to park one at a neighbor's until we could be sure that the Black Hole of Calcutta was fit for human occupancy and until we could find a new mattress. We *said* the old one had been rained on in front of an open window and mildewed, but I don't know whether anyone believed us. In the end it turned out all right. We never saw another bedbug. One teacher left at the end of a month and the other we liked very much indeed. In the spring she married a friend of Ralph's and lived happily ever after—or at least until the present date—in Bangor. Nevertheless for a long time Catherine and I referred to that episode as the worst thing that had ever happened to us in two years of domestic cataclysms. But that was before the Affair of the Ladies' Aid Dishes.

All the small towns I have lived in have a few features in common. They all have a school, a church, a General Store and Post Office—which is also the gossip-swapping center—and they have a Ladies' Aid. The Ladies' Aid in Upton goes so far as to have a little building next door to the church where they give suppers and hold meetings, and it was in this little building that the affair took place. I wasn't there at the time, but I have firsthand reports of it from both Catherine and game warden, Leon Wilson, and I have second-hand reports *ad nauseam* from everyone in Upton.

This is Catherine's version. She sent the boys, her Vaughn and my Rufus, out to play and told them not to go anywhere except the yard and the back pasture. At suppertime she whistled them in, and they came wallowing through the deep snow from the direction of the pasture. "You're good boys," she told them—and that is what burns her up. "To think I actually *praised* the little so-and-so's!"—"You're good boys to stay where I told you." Then she started to help them take off their snowy ski-clothes. To her amazement, in spite of the sub-zero weather, the clothes were warm and soaking wet.

"We were cold," Vaughn told her. "We went over to the Ladies' Aid and started a fire."

Catherine began to put on her jacket and overshoes. Like all of us in the country, she is afraid of fire, and she thought she'd better go over and see that everything was all right. Just then the warden blew in and said he'd go with her, since the early dark of winter had fallen and he had a flash-light, a thing she didn't possess. When the boys saw that she really was going, they volunteered a bit hesitantly that she might possibly find a few broken dishes over there. She gave them a preliminary bawling out, and set out for the Ladies' Aid building, squired by the warden.

Her story from there on is a bit incoherent, but the warden's isn't. He showed up at Forest Lodge the next week and told us about it. They were relieved, he said, to find the building still standing with no signs of smoke arising from it, but just to be sure, they went in the unlocked door. He turned his flashlight on and said, "Jee-*sus!*" The entire floor was littered six inches deep with broken crockery. The overhead lights were smashed, seven panes of glass had been knocked out of the windows, and the teakettle was full of kerosene. The kids had had a heyday, what I mean.

"I wanted to laugh," he said, "but I didn't dare. Catherine would have killed me. She started to cry, and then she'd stop and start to swear. Then she'd cry. God, I never saw such a sight."

I'll bet he never did. The Ladies' Aid had had a complete dinner service for thirty, and there wasn't a whole piece left.

At this point in the narration Ralph started to swear, too.

"Look," I said. "Getting mad won't do any good. I know it was terrible of them, but you'd probably have done the same at their age."

"That's just it, damn it!" he said. "I've always wanted to get into a greenhouse with a bag of stones. We've got to pay for this. We might at least have had some of the fun."

I ignored that and asked Leon, "What happened next?"

"Well, she finally got herself together and picked up a couple of plates that weren't too far gone to eat off of. The kids are using them now, by the way, and they have to explain to everyone that comes in just why. I think that hurts them more than the lickings she gave them." He laughed.

"Boy, she tanned their hides, and I don't blame her. After she got through she walked up and down the kitchen, raving. Miss Hawes"—she was the surviving teacher—" had just been to Berlin and brought home a bunch of celery, because she loves it and they hadn't had any all winter. It was lying on the table and every time Catherine went by, she'd grab a piece off and eat it as if she were chewing the kids' bones. She ate the whole bunch and doesn't remember a thing about it. Poor Hawsey never got a bite. By God I wanted to laugh, but I still didn't dare. You aren't popular in Upton right now."

I could well believe it. It was time, I could see, for Ralph and me to go to Upton and mend our fences, a matter best accomplished by viewing the damage and making replacements.

It was wartime, remember, and things were not as they had been. The broken dishes were all mail-order items, and all unavailable for the duration. It took me from November until April to find dishes to replace the broken ones, and then they were twice as good and three times as expensive as the originals. But I finally got them. The day that I delivered them at the Ladies' Aid building, in committee with one of the Ladies to see that all was correct, was the only time in the whole fracas that I got mad. I unpacked the dishes, allowing her to inspect them individually and microscopically, put them on the shelves, and said, "There!" That "There!" wrote *finis* in my mind to all the talk about our undisciplined and destructive children, all the oblique implications that it was about time I did something more than write letters about getting the dishes, in case the Aid wanted to get up a supper, all the futile letters I'd had to write to china dealers—all the whole irritating, nagging mess.

The Lady looked wistful. "Do you know," she said, "with everyone leaving town, I doubt very much if there'll ever be another supper given by the Aid."

She doesn't know how near death stood to her in that moment. I don't know why I didn't sweep the shelves clean again of dishes, and jump up and down on them on the floor. But I didn't. And the Lady was right. There never has been another supper given there. On the other hand, our children have never wantonly broken another dish, so maybe something was gained.

The rest of Upton wasn't so bad. I'll admit I'm slightly unbalanced about the place. But I wrote the best short story of my life there, sitting at a battered oak desk, pounding it out on a wreck of a typewriter that belonged to Jim's son Gordon, and at intervals policing my young, chatting with the neighbors, and looking out of the window at Umbagog, seven hundred feet below and a mile away. Catherine had gone to the West Coast to kiss her warring husband farewell, and I was holding the fort for her. While I was there the snow faded and the green grass appeared and the evenings were hazy and aromatic with the smoke of pastures being burned off. The best dandelion greens I ever saw sprouted in the barnyard and I dug them by the bushel and shoved them down all the throats that were dependent upon me for sustenance. I could see the steamer *Diamond* trying to hold a boom against the wind, six miles up Umbagog, and the streak of white that meant Ralph was on his way down in the Chriscraft to call on his wife. On Mother's Day he brought me a bunch of flowers he'd picked on the way up Hampshire Hill, and I said, "What's this in favor of?"

"Well, you're a mother, aren't you?" he asked, and sure enough I was, come to think of it. It's an odd thing that while you are aware day and night of the existence of your children, you do forget that Mother's Day is supposed to be for you, too, as well as for Whistler's Mother. Somehow it doesn't seem right for a woman in blue denim slacks and a plaid shirt to be getting flowers, along with all the fragile ancient ladies in black bombazine (whatever that is) and precious lace.

So I said, "Well, thank you, darling," and put them into a jelly glass full of water, where they promptly died. Then we went down and pumped out the bilge in the Chris-craft, installed the new tacometer, and shifted the batteries. I suppose when my children try to get romantic, in their middle age, about the memory of their mother, they're going to be badly stymied. It'll be hard to get too mellow and sentimental about a woman whom they'll remember as always having lubricating grease up to her eyebrows, a fairly powerful overhand stroke, a nice way with dogs, and nothing much else to recommend her, unless you count the ability to climb trees and stone chimneys barefooted.

Andover was the second station in our search for an education. I can't be fair about Andover. I moved out there the day after Ralph died and I was not then, nor for many months later, in any frame of mind to appreciate the town. We had what is known hereabouts as "a good rent"—that is, a nice little house with modern conveniences, and what was more important to me, about the only long view in town, up the valley that leads north to the lakes. That valley acted as a flue, and the wind drew down it day and night. They call the corner on which we lived Windy Corner, and weren't they right! Nights, lying in bed, we'd feel the roof lift and quiver, and we'd think about chimney fires and smell nonexistent smoke. Then we'd get up and prowl and listen to the "Milkman's Serenade," a radio program that lasts from midnight until dawn. As the hours wore on and the announcer got more tired, he got more and more informal. He was good. I grew to like him very much. I used to think about him a lot, sitting there alone, unable to sleep, with the wind pouring down the valley and bombarding Windy Corner. I thought about all the people like me who were too griefstricken to sleep, and all those who were ill, sleepless and restless, and all the nightwatchmen and graveyard shifters, all the men and women with lonely night jobs, who had no one to talk to, no one they could call up at that ungodly hour—all the people who were listening to the "Milkman's Serenade." I wondered if this Art Ford knew what he was doing when he said in the middle of a record, "Ah, the heck with it!" and took it off; or at the end of a record, "Not so bad. Guess we'll have it again." Maybe he didn't care. Maybe he was only putting in time himself. But he made me feel, I think he made us all feel, that in spite of the visible evidence, we were not individually the only persons left alive on a black, bleak earth. I thought once, when I was in New York that winter, I'd stop in at the station and ask him about it, and tell him how many times he and I had sat together through "Drinking Rum and Coca-Cola" and "Sentimental Journey," two current favorites. But I didn't get around to it, and probably he has too many callers already, anyhow.

Although I was in no frame of mind to be easily entertained by anything in Andover, I was entertained in spite of myself now and then. I was entertained by the rivalry between the two women's organizations, the Sisterhood and the Ladies' Aid. They met on alternate weeks, and if the Sisterhood had a chicken-pie supper, the Ladies' Aid, the next week, had a better one. If the Aid raised twenty dollars for some Good Cause, the Sisters raised twenty-two. That's all right—just healthy competition. What amused me was that the membership of the two groups was almost identical —the same people belonged to both, almost to a woman. But I suppose that's no sillier than golf, another game where you spend your time trying to beat your own score.

Someone told me once that you didn't rate socially in Andover unless you'd been in jail. This is not true, of course. Andover is a nice town where a great many very nice people live. During the short while I was there, everybody was very kind and considerate, and I appreciate it very much. But my informant drew his erroneous conclusion from the fact that once some young blade-about-town got into a little trouble and was slapped into the county pokey over at South Paris. Hardly had the cell door clanged behind him than the mail was clogged with post cards for him. The women of Andover had organized a post-card shower to show, I suppose, that their sympathies lay with him in his hour of travail. I'd never heard of such a thing; or am I hopelessly behind the times?

In Andover there is an institution called the Liar's Bench. In summer it is a long bench outside Ike Mills's store, on which any males who aren't at work at the moment foregather to sit and gossip. It's full on summer evenings. As soon as the weather begins to get snappy, come along the end of September, it's moved inside and the self-styled liars sit the winter out around the potbellied stove, from all accounts still gossiping. It's almost a Lodge, and it's as much as any woman's life is worth to get any information out of a Liar as to what has been discussed on the Bench. I know one or two women whose husbands are frequenters, and once in a while I can get a little dirt out of them—if the husbands happen to have been in an expansive mood when they arrived home from a session.

Only once did I have a full account of what took place during a long, snowy, blustery afternoon, and I must say I was intrigued. Doc Stuart, who lives in Andover in the winter, dropped by the house on his way home from the Bench to see how we were and to pass the time of day. He sat down on the wood box in the kitchen, where Catherine and I were busying ourselves, and sighed deeply. "I've had a hard afternoon," he said. "Been at it since two o'clock till just now, when Ike closed up the store for supper."

"At what?" I asked. I'd been at the store earlier and observed no more exhausting activity than settin' and gabbin' entails.

"Hadn't no more'n got over there when Marion Bodwell come in, and after she'd gone the question of her maiden name come up. Every man jack of us knew it as well as we know our own. She's lived here most of her life. But to think of it we couldn't. Spent the whole afternoon rackin' what we call our brains. Tires a man out."

"Why didn't you call her up or ask someone who came in?"

"Didn't seem like it was fair. We was bound and determined to think of it ourselves, since we'd started it." He sighed again. "Had to give up, though, when Ike closed the store. Had to call up the telephone office and ask Katherine McCallister. Minute she said it—Robinson, it was—it come to us like a flash." He rose and pulled on his mittens. "Got to go home and rest."

If there's anything you want to know in Andover, you call up Central, a simple switchboard in a little candy, paper, and ice cream store. Is school going to keep to-day? Is the stage in? Has Larry come out from the lakes yet? Where is Charles Ripley living now? Would the Dixons sell the Sueter house? Anything at all—they'll tell you. Once when Washington was trying to get hold of me at Middle Dam, before Ralph died and I left the lakes, they told the Washington operator to hold on. I'd just gone by in Larry's beach wagon and it wouldn't take me more'n a minute to get to the house I'd rented, whither I was doubtless bound to see my children. And sure enough, I'd no sooner set foot on the porch than the call came through. That's service, of the Andover brand.

It's hard to explain what I feel about Rumford Point, our third and present Outside residence. Several times in the past decade I have passed through the place, with never the slightest thought in my head that I might someday be living here, and I have remarked that I thought it was one of the prettiest little New England villages I ever saw. I've seen villages which have been sold down the river to the summer trade and are self-conscious to the eyebrows, with broad village greens, well-kept Colonial façades, and the A&P disguised as a Tory Tavern. They are lovely, as well-done stage sets are apt to be. Rumford Point has old white houses and wine-glass elms and a beautiful austere church, too, but the town doesn't let them get it down. It has other things on its mind, and its appearance is only incidental. I suppose what I'm getting at—and I hate to use the word because it always sounds so patronizing—is that Rumford Point is unspoiled.

There is the main highway passing through, and the houses are strung along it, set back under tall old trees. On the west is the broad sweep of the Androscoggin, and far away beyond its slow curves, up a long open valley vista, are the White Mountains, untouchable and shining. On the other side of the narrow tree-roofed bench, on which the village lies, stands the long steep wall of Cole Mountain. There are the General Store and Post Office (combined), the fire station, the school and the church, for public buildings. And I guess that's all, except for the ferry. Let me tell you about the ferry.

The first day we came out here to live, I went upstairs to make my choice among the rooms. I would take, I decided, a little room on the back of the house, with a view of the mountains, and the river within spitting distance below its window. I guess maybe one of the reasons I didn't like Andover as well as some other places, come to think of it, was that there was no water to look at. I've lived so long on lake or river that a landscape without water is a pretty pointless affair. But that wasn't the real reason I chose that room. I chose it because it didn't overlook the main highway. There were cars streaming up and down all the time and I, who had hardly seen a car in five months, knew very well that I would spend my time leaning out of the window watching them, rather than leaning over the typewriter as I should be doing. Everyone agreed that this was a wise decision.

The next morning, bright and early, I went to work, pounding stuff out like nobody's business. Pretty soon I heard a clatter and a hooting out on the river, and as I live and breathe, a thing like a scow, only more rickety and railed on the sides, was crossing with two cars aboard. It drew up on the opposite shore—naturally I was practically falling out of the window by this time—and the cars debarked and rolled away. It was an honest-to-God ferry, running back and forth on a cable and powered by a four cylinder Chevrolet motor; so I spent the fall watching it in-

stead of the cars. But the ferry did shut up shop the day the
river froze and the cars on the highway ran all winter, so
there was a net gain.

It is captained by a man whom we knew for a time only as
"Dinah's Easter Bunny." That's who she said he was. I
looked out one day and saw the ferry crossing to pick up a
car on the other side. There, leaning nonchalantly over the
rail with her feet crossed, was my darling infant daughter,
having a sail for herself. When she got home, I told her she
wasn't supposed to ride on the ferry. You had to give the
man money to do that, and she didn't have any money. She
said she didn't either need money; her Easter Bunny invited
her to ride. This we couldn't quite follow, since the ferry-
man didn't look to us like any bunny. He looks like a
countryman of indeterminate age. So we put it down to one
of childhood's delightful fancies. But it turned out that his
name is Mr. Easter, and we still refer to him occasionally as
Dinah's Easter Bunny.

Well do I remember the day of the ferry's last run of the
season. At five o'clock in the morning, a few days after
Thanksgiving, I was awakened by what can only be called a
hubbub. Car horns were blowing, men were shouting, and
some of the most inspired swearing I'd heard in a long time
was being executed. I piled out of bed and hung out the
window. The searchlight on the ferry and the lights of a
couple of cars gave the scene a weird, exaggerated clarity.
Our shore of the Androscoggin was in darkness, and so were
the fields and ridges beyond the other shore. But the ferry
and the black, slickly flowing surface of the water about it
were illuminated brilliantly. Floating cakes of ice, known as
anchor-ice, were charging down the current, and Mr. Easter,
armed with a boat hook, was struggling manfully to keep

them out of his motor and propeller, which are slung amidships on the upstream side of the ferry. He was not working silently either. For a rather small man, he has a very carrying voice, and I was left with no doubt whatsoever as to his opinion of the state of affairs generally. It then developed under my fascinated gaze that the landing beach was plugged with ice, too, so Mr. Easter and the cars aboard the ferry were marooned.

In the meantime Dinah's Easter Bunny was as busy as a bird dog. He would fend off a cake of ice, pause to wipe his face, and shout to a car which was hopefully honking on our side of the river, "No use of you honking. I can't get over and I can't get back. You gotta go 'round!" Going 'round means the ten-mile trip to Rumford, for the first bridge below here, or the thirteen-mile trip to Bethel for the first bridge above. More ice-parrying and more shouting to would-be passengers. This went on all morning. Then somehow when my back was turned, he got off, heaven knows how. I looked out and there was the ferry, still stuck offshore with cars aboard; but Rufus came in and announced that Mr. Easter was just walking past the house. A man does have to get home for lunch, after all, even if it means doing an Eliza on a mess of loose ice and bumming a ride all the way 'round. After lunch a tractor appeared on the other shore and dragged the ferry in through the ice to the landing, and that was that. Mr. Easter issued the pronouncement that if he ever got the gol-danged thing back across the river, he'd haul her out for the winter that very day, by God. And by God, he did.

But you know, he misses her. All this winter I've seen him at intervals go past the house—we live on the corner of the ferry road—to assure himself that his command was all right. And just the other morning, at an unholy hour, I heard the sound of pounding. The snow was almost off and the ice was almost out, and Mr. Easter was down getting everything shipshape for his summer voyaging.

It's not only the physical appearance of the town that I like; it's the people, too. I know you can't take a population of sixty people and love them all dearly and equally. That's silly. Some of them I don't even know, some I know only slightly, and some, naturally, I like better than others. What I mean is that I like the common outlook and the accepted values and standards of the people here. There is a nice feel about the place. I think I myself am responsible to a certain extent for my own feeling in this matter. When I came here to live last fall, it was to be the first time in twelve years that I had lived in a community larger than Middle Dam (pop. 11). Andover didn't count. I wasn't there for a full year and I wasn't myself. And I'd never spent more than a few days in Upton when the kids went to school there.

Shortly after I got here, I got into a discussion with my next-door neighbors, Charles and Virginia Hutchins, about civic responsibility. Charles and I were agreed that if you were to live in a community for any length of time you owed both it and yourself a certain amount of interest and participation in community affairs. It's axiomatic that you get out of anything—a place, a personal relationship, a project of any sort—only as much as you put into it. But it works the other way, too. Rumford Point has put a lot into me, in the way of kindnesses and friendliness, and I hope it has got something out of me in return.

Virginia, who besides being my neighbor is my friend, claims she feels no sense of civic obligation at all. But we hadn't been in the house half an hour, the day we moved here, when she brought us up a chocolate cake and a pan of hot rolls for our supper. She'd never laid eyes on us before, either. She says this was only simple and decent neighborliness, but I think possibly one thing is an extension of the other.

Another thing, besides Virginia's chocolate cake and the discovery of the ferry, happened the first few days that we were out here in Rumford Point to predispose me in its favor. I had to know our address, in the interests of filling out Rufus' school registration card, so I went out and shouted up to a man who was fixing our roof, "Hey, what's the name of this street?"

He looked at me from the superior height of the ridgepole, spat over his shoulder, and said, "Hell, lady, this ain't no street. This is just a road." He pronounced "road" the Maine way, halfway between "rode" and "rud." It can't be conveyed phonetically, and nobody unless to the manner born can really say it properly. I've been practicing on it for twelve years, and I haven't got it down right yet. However, no matter how you pronounce it, I feel more at home living on a road than on a street. I am by inheritance, background, training, disposition, and free choice, a hick.

Maybe that's why I like the store so much. Everyone knows all about country stores, and this one is no different from the rest. The stock consists of practically everything, from cement to Marshmallow Fluff to wool shirts to flashlights. There is a wood-burning stove down toward the rear, with a bench alongside for the convenience of the public; because, of course, the store is as much a club as a mart of trade. One of the front corners is Holy Ground, being partitioned off by a wall of glass-fronted pigeonholes and serving as the Post Office. This brings it under Federal juris-

diction and no one except Johnny, or his agents Helen and
Mr. Hall, is allowed back there. I used to call Johnny and
Helen, Mr. and Mrs. Martin, but I was the only one in
town who did; and besides, he's my landlady's son, as well
as being proprietor of the store, so I felt as though I were being slightly ostentatious. At mail time Johnny is in the Post
Office, distributing mail through a little window, but if you
go in between mail times he is apt to be down at the other
end of the store, weighing out nails or sacking up potatoes.
Most people have to wait until he is through to get their
letters, but a few of us lucky ones have pigeonholes near
enough the distribution window so that by thrusting an arm
in, bending it at an awkward and painful angle, and scratch-
ing like crazy with our fingernails, we can extract our own
mail from our boxes. I have a vague impression that this
may be against postal law, so, every time I do it, I feel just
like Jesse James. It adds more zest to the already zestful experience of getting letters to wonder if that stranger in the
store-bought clothes who is posing as a seed salesman
mightn't really be a member of the FBI, just panting to
pounce. I am, I admit freely, easily entertained.

But that's not the real story about the store. I guess I
can't tell the real story. I only know that one day in January
I set out to get my milk and mail. It was about nine o'clock
in the morning and I'd been too busy to notice that there
was a blizzard raging. I put on my old tweed coat, my overshoes, and the square of cloth that I use for a hat, and sallied
forth. I waded knee deep through the drift that always
blocks our doorway, stamped myself indignantly onto the
highway, discovered that even there, there wasn't plain sailing, and, boots full of snow, battled a sleet-ladened wind the
hundred yards to my destination. I don't know why I was so

mad. I guess it was for the same reason that a wet hen or a wet cat gets mad.

Then I opened the door of the store and stepped out of the storm into a pool of calm. It was quiet and shadowy in there, with the silence broken only by the whispering of the sleet against the dim windows, the snapping of the fire in the rosy stove, and the slow, deep, unhurried, country voices of the men who were there. There was no business being done. Johnny and Mr. Hall were leaning on the counter, and four or five other men, kept from work by the weather, were sitting on the bench. They were talking about other storms in other times, and there was an attitude of acceptance, of unresentful recognition of superior force, that was as elemental as the storm itself. It was snowing and blowing, but nothing could be done about it, so why get upset?

"Quite a storm, Mis' Rich," said one. "Reckon by night we'll see two feet. She's starting in just like she did in '98."

"Now there was a real blizzard. I remember I was just setting out for Bangor——"

I don't remember much about it all, but I stayed and listened to the talk for a while, and when I went out, I felt good. Don't ask me why. I just did. I took Virginia's milk and mail and went down to her house to deliver it, enjoying now, because I felt so fine, the cut of the wind and the strange, rare odor of snow, which is like no other odor on earth.

"Do you know, Gina," I said, "I guess I'm nuts, but I just love living in a place where you can go into the store in your old rags and talk about the blizzard of '98. And what's so wonderful about that?"

She said, "I don't know. But I feel exactly the same way."

I guess maybe she's one of the reasons I love living in Rumford Point. She always sees my point of view, and most of the time she shares it. You can have a certain amount of fun alone, anywhere, but the same things are four times as much fun if you can count on someone laughing at the same things you laugh at, catching your most oblique references, and thinking the same things are important or sad. Virginia agreed with me that Johnny's attitude the day we went over to take some pictures of the store was an index to the character of the town. We persuaded him and Mr. Hall and two or three other men to come out and stand on the steps, and we took their pictures. When it was all over, Johnny said ruefully, "If I'd known about this beforehand, I'd have tidied up the porch. Looks kind of slack, the way it is."

Maybe it did look slack to Johnny, but Johnny's like the rest of the town. He doesn't put on an act about being a real Yankee storekeeper. He's too busy being one to recognize the atmospheric value of a molasses barrel and a bunch of snow shovels on the porch. I've seen storekeepers in the tourist zone who'd skin you alive if you suggested tidying up their stage properties.

Then we have the V.I.S. That stands for Village Improvement Society and the chief purpose of the organization is to raise money for fire protection. We have a little fire station and a fire truck, and the manpower is purely volunteer. When the bell rings, every male in town drops what he's doing and runs to fight the fire. Even so, it takes money to run the outfit, so, during the winter, whist parties are held, each person in town taking his turn at being host. Each guest contributes as entry fee whatever he can, over and above fifteen cents. So a certain amount of money is raised, but more important than that, a social occasion is provided for a town that hasn't even a one-night-a-week movie.

Along about February, Virginia said to me, "How about it, Civic-minded? They're looking for someone to give the V.I.S. party this month."

Well, after all, I had said I believed in public-spiritedness—and she, who'd said she didn't, had given the party the month before—so I said, "All right. How do I go about it?"

The way you go about it is to take a piece of paper and write on it—unless you can print: "V.I.S. Whist Party, Thursday, February 14 at 8 o'clock at Louise Rich's House." This you take over to the store and tack up on the trim of the front showcase, after having bummed a couple of tacks from Johnny for the purpose. Then you go home and start worrying about what you'll have to eat, and where you'll get enough chairs and tables for the assemblage—supposing anyone comes—and what you'll do about dishes and packs of cards.

You can spare yourself the worry, because everyone will come, and everyone will lend you anything he owns to promote the occasion. You can get chairs and card tables from the schoolhouse, and Elton Knight, the President of the V.I.S., and Virginia's husband, Charles, will go over and get them for you and return them after the party. Virginia will let you have all her good cups and saucers and plates, and help you make sandwiches. Two or three other women will call up and offer to bring additional sandwiches, just in case you run short. Briefly, you may say that you are giving the party, but it's really a community affair. I never was the object of so much friendly coöperation in my life as I was the day I gave the V.I.S. Whist Party. Twenty-four people came, and I've given parties for four, before now, that were a lot more work and worry. I'd dreaded the thing ever since I'd said I'd do it, but as Virginia commented after it was over and we were doing the dishes while Charles ate the left-over ice cream, "I never had so much fun at an ordeal in my life!"

Life at Rumford Point isn't one long idyll, of course. Life at any point on the globe that you care to mention isn't a long idyll. Some bad things and some sad things have happened to me here. Catherine left me, for one thing, because her husband was discharged from the service and our original agreement was that she'd stay for the duration. I miss her, naturally, after four years. And I miss Vaughn. Every time we have ripe olives I remember that he ate thirty-nine—on top of everything else—last Thanksgiving. After the twelfth, we decided to see, in the interests of science, just how far he'd go, given a free rein. He didn't even get sick. Youth is wonderful.

And then I had to have Kyak killed. He was old and sick and in frightful pain, and I have no sympathy with the kind of sentimentality which calls itself love, and yet will allow an animal to go through the tortures of the damned, just because it hurts like blazes to order his death. That isn't love. Kyak had been with us since his birth nine years ago. He'd slept every night by the side of my bed, gone wherever we went, bounced around like a fool when he knew we were happy, and whined and worried and tried to comfort us when he knew we were not. He'd sat all night with me through the long black hours after Ralph died and I was alone until dawn. When I buried Ralph's ashes in the place where he wanted them buried, Kyak alone was with me. Don't tell me that dogs are soulless. I know better. There are some things that I never could have accomplished with the dignity that everyone owes himself, if it hadn't been for the dignity of my dog, supporting me, setting me an example. He was a good dog. He was my friend in a world where loyal friends are hard-come-by. So I did for him the friendliest thing I knew how to do. I arranged that he should meet death while he still could do so with integrity.

But then I thought, "Children should grow up with a dog, and the time to get a new dog is while your heart is still sore for the old. I guess I'll buy the kids a puppy for Christmas." And that was one more mistake in a life well studded with mistakes. I went to a kennel, intent on getting one pup, and I came home with three. First I saw an airedale that I loved; he was so square and tough and homely. Then I saw his twin brother; and I couldn't bear to part them. Then I saw a little English springer spaniel that looked like a small girl's dog. So I decided to give each child—Vaughn, Rufus, Dinah—a dog for Christmas, and call it a day. Well, Vaughn's dog is gone, now, but we still have Patches and Doggone. Patches is Dinah's dog, the springer, and he is named Patches because after Santa Claus left the North Pole and was flying high in the sky over the swamps of Canada, a hunter mistook him for a flock of ducks and let go with his shotgun. Santa Claus looked, and there was this white dog he'd picked out for Dinah, all full of holes. He didn't have time to go back and get a replacement, so he said, "Golly, I'll have to patch him up somehow." All he had for material was an old black fur robe, so he cut some pieces out of that and stuck them over the holes—and there was a black-and-white dog named Patches. About Doggone—he was intended for a smug little girl with close-set eyes, long golden curls, and a mean disposition. Santa told him about his new intended owner, and he said, "Well, doggone, if I'll live with her!" in the stubborn way that airedales have. Santa said,

"Well, Doggone, if that's the way you feel about it—" and he brought him to Rumford Point, and he's Rufus' dog, Doggone! Or at least that's Ma's version of the transaction.

I guess we'd better skip Ma's version of the six weeks following Christmas. It's hard enough to housebreak one winter pup, but three! How can you decide whose nose to rub in what, unless you see the act perpetrated? Oh well, that's over now. Doggone and Patches are reasonably well-trained dogs. I hope!

Then I've had the trouble of the plants. When we took over the house, my landlady, Lyle Martin, had some very nice house plants in pots around the porch. I said, "What do you want me to do about them?" and she said, "Oh, don't bother with them." But there was a certain wistful something in her eye. Then I said, "That Lobster Cactus looks a little yellow and washed up," and she said, "So would you, if you were as old as that plant. It was my great-grandmother's." Well, after all! To let old age like that die in a snowdrift would be sacrilege. So I said, "I'll take them in and tend them. I like house plants, anyhow," just as if I'd ever had anything to do with one. She gave me such a skeptical look that I determined then and there to keep the things alive until spring if I had to cut my wrists and water them with my life blood. And I pretty nearly have had to, but they are—to date—alive and reasonably well. And I'll admit that when the snow was blowing by the windows so thick that I couldn't see across the road, and the drifts were head high, it was worth the tending and fussing to have something green and fresh in the living-room. *And* the yellow, washed-out cactus did crash through with three blossoms on the night of the V.I.S. party.

My present trouble is the Trouble of the Tole Tray. I

now claim, quite unfairly, that Virginia sucked me into
this. She didn't. I offered, my-own-self, to do it. Virginia
has on many occasions made life bearable for me, so the
least I could do for her, I thought, was do over this old tray
she had. And I will, by the gods. It's a lovely shape, and
will make a lovely tray, if I'm lucky. The thing is, there is
more to making a tole tray than just slapping some paint
onto it. If it's an old tray, as this is, you have to remove all
the rust and old paint. This I have done. Then you have
to have the proper black matt surface, which is achieved
by using Japanese lamp black, not now available. But
Thurston Cole, up the road, had a very good substitute,
which he let me borrow. I have two coats of that on the tray,
at the moment, and will put a third on this afternoon.
Thurston also lent me a book on how to do tolework. My
spirits sank when I read it. You have to have fancy materials
and a special technique, neither of which I had any idea
how to acquire. But Leo Cyr, in Rumford, had all the necessary powdered bronzes and peacock blues, which he was
nice enough to lend me. He also gave me a book on how to
do tolework—which would have been all right, except that
it doesn't agree with Thurston's book. Leo's contention is
that one may use any method at all, even a blow torch, just
so long as the final result looks like old tole. Thurston's
creed is that the method is as important as the end, so we
use only the tools available a hundred years ago. This leaves
me in a fix, for I will state quite frankly that I know nothing at all about the subject.

"Don't let that bother you," Virginia advised me airily.
"Get one of them to do it for you, and then you can show
it to the other to prove how smart you are. You can't lose.
And neither can I," she added. "After all, no matter who

does it, I get the tray." So I guess this week is going to be National Tole Tray Week.

There is a lot more I could say about Rumford Point, but it all adds up to the same thing. I like it here. About a month ago, before the ice was out of the Androscoggin, I was paddling across the road into the yard on my way home from getting the mail, when I was accosted by a car with a New York license plate, coming up from the ferry. In it were two dapper gentlemen with irritated sneers on their faces. "We thought," they said nastily, "that there was a ferry here."

"Well, there is," I told them. "But the river is frozen, as you can see, so naturally it can't run."

"How do you expect us to get across to Rumford Corners?" they demanded, as if I gave a damn whether they got across or not. "A fine thing! Ferry's marked right here on the map, and you pull it out for the winter. That's the native for you."

"If you want to get across to the Corners," I said, "you'll have to go to Bethel and take the bridge there." It would have been three miles shorter for them to have gone by way of Rumford, which is not so much of a difference.

But the point is this. Right then I knew, once and for all, that I had identified myself for good with the "natives." Outsiders can't come in and criticize us with impunity; not while I still have breath to send them the long way around. I was being childish, of course; it was a silly and petty thing for me to do. But there's nothing silly in knowing where you belong. There's nothing childish in throwing in your lot, for better or for worse, with the people in the places that you love.

CHAPTER X

The Little Things

MUCH AS I hate to employ stock phrases, since they always seem to me to have been sapped of import through years of weary usage, I do find myself giving utterance occasionally to some such gem from the accumulated treasure of the ages as "It's the little things that count." The dismaying part of this is that—annoyed with myself as I may be for thus having fallen back on banality and sure as I am that just because a thing has been said four million and thirty-seven times it is not necessarily true—in this case I can't think up a better or more succinct way of expressing what is at least the part of a truth. Of course, it is actually the big things that count. But when the big things counterbalance, it's the little things which decide the issue. When a problem comes up of decision between the friend who is loyal, steadfast, and trustworthy and the friend who is truly all this and charming as well, the charming friend wins. Charm, so called for want of a better word, is a little thing, weighed in the balance of true worth. We all know charming heels. But such little things do tip the scales.

So when I try to weigh the life I lead in the woods against any other life I might lead, balancing freedom of action and thought, lack of social and time pressure, and a feeling of entity, against the restrictions placed upon my mobility here by the weather and the seasons, lack of opportunity to keep abreast of trends, and unarguable physical hardship—even danger—imposed upon us all, I have to turn to the little things. There are little things against my staying here— little things like chapped hands with broken nails, a tendency on the part of my young to do it the easy way and say "ain't," lack of plumbing, cold rooms in which to dress on sub-zero mornings, and a sickening ennui, along-come February, with canned meat, salt fish and baked beans as staples of diet. But there are also little things on the side of not giving it up in favor of a small steam-heated apartment with oceans of hot running water, movies around the corner, sophisticated cocktail parties, and the best school in the world on the next block. Let me tell you some of the things. They aren't particularly important, but they make all the difference to me.

There was the time, for example, that we went over to B Pond to put Frank Richardson's canoe under cover. We woke to a gray November dawn and ate breakfast by lamplight in the warm kitchen. While Ralph and I were drinking our second cups of coffee, I asked, "What's on the docket for to-day?"

"I told Frank I'd get his canoe in before snow fell, and the time's running short, so I guess I'll do that to-day. Why don't you come, too?"

"Yes," I said, tartly, because I wanted so much to go. "And leave Rufus to tend fires and get his own lunch, I suppose."

"He's four. It's only a mile over the ridge. He can come, too."

So we banked the fire, put on heavy clothes, whistled

the dog, and set out up the road and across the dam just as the east glowed with a sulphurous yellow through the low-hung clouds. Our ears were full of the sound of churning water as we went single file along the narrow walkway, but when we left the end of the dam-fill and started up the trail over the ridge, the sound fell behind us and dimmed and died. It was lovely in the woods that morning, as peaceful and hushed as a cathedral. The fir and spruce and pine stood up tall over our heads, their tips motionless against the sky, and the beech, still clinging to their faded leaves, glowed pale gold against the dark of the evergreens. The ground was carpeted with fallen birch and maple leaves, showing bright through the white of last night's sprinkling of hoarfrost. Ralph went first, then Rufus, then I brought up the rear, while Kyak galloped ahead or deployed on mysterious missions of his own. At the height of land, two deer sprang out of a thicket and jumped a windrow of blow-down, their white flags flying high and brave as they disappeared from sight. Rufus stood stock-still, his face ecstatic, and something swift and congratulatory passed between Ralph and me over his unconscious head. So we came down the last steep pitch to the pond.

The canoe lay right side up, half-full of ice-skimmed water. Ralph looked at her. "Someone ought to be shot. We'll have to bail her out. We'll rack hell out of her if we try to dump her." We found some old tin cans in Frank's camp and started bailing.

After a minute I looked at Rufus' little hands, turning slowly raw and purple, and the mother's heart in me spoke. "You don't have to help, dear. Put your mittens back on and watch."

"I like to help," he said gruffly; so I said no more. We

bailed down to within two inches of the bottom and dumped her. Ralph took the bow and Rufus and I the stern—I could have managed better alone—and we carried her into camp. Then we sat down to rest.

"Working makes a man hungry," Rufus commented. "I'm starved."

I looked around the camp. There was tea and canned beans and milk and crackers on the shelf. "Frank wouldn't mind if we built a fire and had lunch here," I suggested.

We ate and drank out of tin cups and plates. Even Rufus had a little tea in a cup of sweetened, diluted canned milk. We grew hilarious over the meal, telling each other about all the things we'd do together in the future, now that Rufus was old enough to go, too. We had a good time in that little one-room shack, sitting on bare benches and eating from the plank table. Then we washed the dishes, put out the fire, locked the camp, and started home.

The day had changed. Where we walked on the forest floor the air was still hushed, but the wind was in the tops of the trees, roaring with a dull muffled roar. The sky hung low and dark. The dog kept to our heels, subdued by some atavistic fear, and we saw no sign of life, not even a snow-bird. The world seemed to be holding its breath and waiting—for what, we couldn't tell.

It struck us just as we came off the dam. The roar of the wind changed to a whine and then to a high-pitched shriek and a wall of snow whirled down on us from the north. We staggered before the blow, and Kyak crouched and whimpered, with the curl all gone out of his tail. Then we took hands and started running with the storm pounding at our backs and tearing at our clothes. We burst into the kitchen and slammed the door behind us. We were safe.

"Now," I said, "you poke the fire up, Ralph, and I'll get some supper started. You, Rufus, start undressing——" Then I looked at him, so little and long-past-bedtime, so loath to end his first day of being really grown up. "Or see if you can get something on the radio," I added, moved to compassion.

He twisted the dials of the battery set, and in a minute a smooth voice filled the room. "And now as we draw near the close of this Thanksgiving Day——"

"For Pete's sake!" said Ralph, and we looked at each other and laughed. "You have dopey parents," he told Rufus. "We forgot it was Thanksgiving."

Now I know that's not much of a story, but let me tell you the rest of it. Last year we had a twenty-three pound turkey, served on a white cloth, with all the fixings. Twenty people sat down at the table. It was quite a Thanksgiving. At the end of the meal Rufus said, "That was a good dinner; but, Ma, remember that Thanksgiving when we forgot what day it was? Remember seeing the deer and eating the beans over at B Pond? Gosh"—he sighed with the deep nostalgia of eight for lost youth—"that was the best Thanksgiving I ever had."

I opened my mouth to say something biting about the hours I'd spent preparing a meal that ranked a poor second to a darned old can of store beans, but I closed it again. After all, he was right. That day we'd walked in beauty together. We'd shared work in mutual respect. We'd come home safe through danger to our own roof and our own fire. We'd been truly thankful.

That had been one of the little things I'm talking about.

I like to think about the baseball games at Pine Point,

too. They started one evening after supper, when Doc Stuart was busy with what he termed "spearin' 'round for somethin' to do." He sat on a stone outside the kitchen door and delivered a monologue which wound up, "—or we could play baseball—if we only had a ball and a bat and enough people and a place to play."

"There's an old baseball in that box of toys on the porch," I told him from the window, "and a bat is only a stick of wood, after all. We could play out back of the house." I looked at the open space outside and added a bit doubt-fully, "I guess." It sloped rather steeply from the guides' house to the kitchen door and was covered with long grass, out of which a generous sprinkling of boulders reared their heads. "I'll go see if anyone else wants to play."

Catherine and Doris and Pearl, doing the dishes, all said they'd like a play, although Doris admitted that she'd never even seen a baseball game, since she'd been born, and lived until her family was fortunate enough to escape, in Nazi Germany where baseball evidently simply Wasn't Done. She'd like to learn, she said, if we'd show her how. We said we would, and I went out onto the front porch where the family and guests were assembled in after-supper peace. There was a banker and a lawyer and two editors and a radio-script man, with their assorted wives and husbands, and a game warden, to say nothing of Ralph and a collection of our own and others' young fry. They all thought a base-ball game was a good notion, so we adjourned to the back yard where Doc had collected Whit Roberts and the chore-boy Frank, and was putting the finishing touches on the bat. He was allowed to be one captain, because it was his idea in the first place, and the banker was allowed to be the other, because it turned out that he'd played while at college.

They tossed the bat and caught it, in the tradition-honored fashion, and placed hand above hand along its length to determine who would have first choice of players. Doc won and chose Whit Roberts, whom he had seen play, in years gone, on the Andover Town Team. One of the editors—a lady editor from *Harper's Bazaar*—went last off the block. She didn't look like any bargain on any man's baseball team, with her silk print blouse and her high-piled hair and her fantastic earrings.

That was a baseball game to end all baseball games. We chose one boulder for the home plate and three others, at approximate diamond positions, for the bases. Then we shuttered all the windows on the back of the house, just in case, and went to it. At the end of the first inning the score stood sixteen to sixteen, Ralph had fallen over his own big feet but managed to make the plate on his hands and knees amid agonized shrieks of "Home! Home!" on the part of the opposition; Doris had connected with the ball and hopped up and down imploring, "What'll I do now?"—and we were all weak with laughter, except Whit, who takes his baseball seriously, and the lady from *Harper's Bazaar*. She'd been a terrible shock to us, the enemy. She'd sat on a log smoking quietly until it came her turn to bat. Then she'd stepped to the plate, hitched up her twenty-dollar slacks, spat on her hands in a businesslike manner, and slammed the first ball pitched to her deep into left field. She had, it turned out, played sand-lot scrub all the days of her small-town youth, and her hand and eye had not lost their cunning. Taken by surprise in left field, I muffed the ball, and Whit inquired bitterly whether I wanted a basket. I redeemed myself later by knocking one over the pumphouse roof into the lake. It would have been a home run, only

Frank announced that lost balls and balls in the lake were good for only two bases.

But I finally lost the game for our side anyhow, just as the sun touched the hills of New Hampshire. There was no excuse for it. I was just standing there, paying no heed to what was going on. I was listening to the beautiful sounds of wind in murmuring treetops and water washing on stone. I was looking at the purple hulk of Mount Washington looming up fifty miles to the south through the gold sheen of the sun-shot evening. I was thinking how simply swell it was to live in a place where eighteen people, having widely divergent backgrounds and educations and politics and bank accounts, could take an old ball and a whittled-down stick of wood and have a time for themselves; where a choreboy could lay down a rule we all abided by without question because it was fair and reasonable; where a man could hold up his head and rebuke the boss's wife for clumsiness with no fear of retribution, since the right was on his side. I was deciding that right that minute I wouldn't swap places with anyone in the world, when there was a sharp crack and a ball came sailing like a bullet out of nowhere right at me. I didn't even try to catch it. I just ducked and the game was over.

We played baseball after supper a lot from then on, and it was always fun. It was one of the little things that count.

We pitched horseshoes, too, out in front of the house, on a plot of ground between the porch and the edge of the lake, where the flagpole stands bolted to a boulder and there is a rock with a groove chiseled down the middle of it and the initials "N.H." carved on one side and "ME." on the other. It marks where the old interstate line used to run, in the rough and ready days when state lines were a bit casual.

Had we lived at that time, we could have evaded the local law simply by retiring to the pumphouse with a good book and a box of saltines. As it is, now that the line has been corrected, we'd have to swim fifty yards off shore from the pumphouse landing, there to tread water and hurl defiance as long as our breaths lasted, which wouldn't be too long.

I like to pitch horseshoes. It's a leisurely, sociable, undemanding game, well suited to such lethargic and voluble souls as myself. You don't have to waste your breath running and shouting, but can save it for the much more interesting business of talking. You stand behind one of the stakes, your toe, slightly turned in, firm against it, and swing your arm with a loose, free motion. The horseshoe arcs through the air and lands with a thud near the other stake. Some people hold the shoe by one side and throw it with a back-hand motion. I'm of the school that holds it square in the middle and gives it a flip as it leaves the hand, so that it turns over once, slowly, in flight and comes to ground, ends first, for a ringer—if your judgment of distance and direction happens to have been correct. Then you stand back while your opponent pitches, and together stroll to the other stake and view the results. Sometimes it's a pretty near thing, so you have to pull up a blade of long grass and measure. This shoe and this shoe won't count. You kick them aside. It's between this and this. You both squat solemnly down and tape off the distances with the piece of grass. Your opponent seems to have you by an eighth of an inch, so you pick up your two shoes, whack them together to knock off the loam, and stand back to watch him pitch.

There used to be a game of horseshoes going on most of the time at Pine Point, since it took only two to play and the equipment was right there always, with the shoes nested around the stake between times. It was somehow pleasant to be sitting alone in my room, scowling over a typewriter, and to hear the familiar ringing clang of the shoes. It would go on for a while, interspersed with shouts and laughter, and then there would be silence again and I'd know the game was over, and I'd go back to my work.

I never thought I'd get any fun out of our bats, but in the end I did. At Forest Lodge we have a whole attic full of the things and I hate them. Ralph would never do anything about them, or let me, as he said—probably rightly—that they kept the mosquitoes and midges down. He quoted impressive figures about how many insects one bat ate on an average in one night. I don't remember what the figures were —thousands, if not millions—but if what he said was true, the number of bugs the bats in our attic disposed of could be reckoned only in the figures usually reserved for light years or national debts. I used to lie in bed in the early gray of dawn and hear them squeaking up there over my head as the mothers came home from their night's jaunt and lined up their young. They made a frightful racket, so one day I started up through the trap door in the upstairs-hall ceiling to see for myself what went on. I didn't get very far, because as soon as my chin cleared the attic floor I could see them hanging from the beams in great bunches as big as bushel baskets. The clusters writhed and quivered obscenely, and I withdrew my head and slammed down the door fast. I told Ralph that I wouldn't live in that house with that horrid population conducting its loathsome life within ten feet of me, and he'd better plan to do something about it. So he wrote the Government for instructions for building a bat roost, informing me that the Government had pamphlets on everything. But they didn't have any on bat roosts, it turned out, and I listened to a lecture on the state of a nation that would do a thing like Passamaquoddy and neglect something really vital like providing for bats. Fortunately, before I really had to take a stand, my sister discovered that San Antonio, Texas, has a Municipal Bat Roost. So Ralph wrote the mayor of that enlightened city for plans or at least a description, and I signed an armistice on the subject of bats which was to last until the Middle Dam Municipal Bat Roost should be constructed.

But it never was. Last summer I discovered to my dismay that if I didn't do something about the roof of the main house pretty soon, I wouldn't have a roof. As it was, every time a heavy dew fell, the shout of "Man the battle stations!" would arise, and every member of the family would run with pans and place them under the leaks. We developed quite a routine. Each had his own pans and his own leaks, and in less than a minute we'd be ready for a cloudburst. But that is not, after all, the ideal answer to the problem of a leaky roof. The ideal answer is a roof that doesn't leak.

So I went into a huddle with Whit, who told me that if I was going to do anything about the roof, I might as well do it right. The present roof consisted of cedar shingles nailed onto boards which were spaced about six inches apart in the interests of conserving lumber. If it were his roof, Whit said, he'd rip it all off, shove the boards up tight, piece out with some new boards, and go on from there with the roofing I'd bought. I agreed with him. "And," I added, "while you have the roof off, you and Doc might clean out those damn bats. Then if you're careful about a tight roof, they can't get in again." He said all right.

The next day was what Doc calls "a good-livin' day," with the same inflection with which you speak of a good-lookin' girl or a sweet-runnin' boat, so it was decided at breakfast that that would be roof-and-bat day. There are many nice things about Whit Roberts, and one of the nicest is that he always goes through the formality of asking me what I want done and how I want it done. Naturally I don't know. He's the carpenter; I'm not. So I think it's sweet of him to underwrite gravely every morning at breakfast the pleasant fiction that I am now the boss. We both know the answer, which is, "Well, what do you think, Whit?" He tells me what he thinks, in his quiet authoritative voice, and that's what we do. This morning Whit and Doc climbed up onto the roof with shovels and started shoveling off the shingles, and the rest of us sat in the yard below to see the bats. We didn't have long to wait. As soon as the roof was clear of shingles, the men started ripping boards off, and a great cloud of jittering darkness swirled up like smoke through the opening into the brilliant sunlight.

"Holy Jesus!" said Whit, and ducked. There must have been thousands of the things, bumbling blindly about in the light. We all screamed and ran. By the time we dared stick our noses out of the house again, they had all disappeared—into the tool shed we later found out—and the men were killing the few die-hards who remained in the attic. "Guess we got them all," Whit announced finally, and proceeded to put on a new, hermetical roof, which wouldn't leak in a hundred years, he announced at supper. I won't know for quite a while whether he was right about that; but he wasn't right about getting all the bats. We found that out at about ten that night.

Catherine and I were sleeping in one room, that spell,

because her sister Eva was staying with us and had my room, along with her baby and Dinah. We were all undressed and in bed when Eva shrieked. We piled out, lighted lamps, and rushed in to see what the matter was. We didn't see Eva at all, but a voice from the quivering heap of blankets on the bed spoke one word, "Bats!" She could have saved her breath. We could see them all right—about a dozen of them swishing madly around and around the room in horrible parade.

"Good God!" said Catherine. "Get the brooms." Whit had been all too faithful in making a tight roof, and the few survivors of the pogrom—a bat can crawl into the smallest space imaginable and hide—had been unable to get outdoors. So instead they'd come down into the house.

That was an eerie performance. Catherine and I, armed with the brooms and grim, tight-lipped expressions, swung lustily at equally grim and tight-lipped bats. Every now and then we'd hit one and shout, "I wounded him! Get him, quick!" and Eva would thrust one eye out from under the bedclothes, wail like a banshee, and disappear again. The children slept peacefully through it all, even when Catherine and I were volleying a breathless but dogged bat back and forth across their cribs. Finally I looked at her and she looked at me, between murderous swipes with the brooms, and we both started to laugh. "Crimus, you look funny," she said, and I'm sure I did, because she did, with her hair on end over a cold-creamed face and a pink satin nightgown, a maniacal gleam in her eye, and the broom at the ready in her hand. "There goes another! Get him!" And we got back to business. We eventually got them all. It was quite a sporting evening. I'm not a killer by nature, but that was one kill that I enjoyed. There is something so evil about a bat. Even in extremity he looks at you with such leering malice, drawing back his upper lip in a snarl of pure hate. It's frightening.

There are other small things that I enjoy around here. I like the language of the country, for one thing. I like to hear women speak of "baking off" a batch of bread or giving the living-room a "lick and a promise" until "turning out day." I like "I give him a growl" for "I rebuked him," and "Wind it into you" for "Eat your dinner," and "Soon's he got his feet braced" for "As soon as he became accustomed to conditions," and "He put down the road" for "He scrammed out of there." It isn't cold and bitter on the lake in January, with the wind howling, knife edged, out of the north and the thermometer cringing down to thirty below; it is, simply, "des'prit." And when we're startled by a person's coming suddenly and quietly into a room, we say, "My, you jumped me!" We don't wander heedlessly and carelessly into a room, knocking over occasional tables and smashing bric-a-brac; we come "gawmin' along." And we don't spend warm spring afternoons daydreaming in the sun; we "set and numb."

To me these expressions mean something. They are accurately descriptive, not only of facts but of mood. I will not say that they are quaint and picturesque, because they are not in the shopworn sense of those patronizing adjectives. They are of the indigenous tongue of the people, springing from accurate observation, kept alive because they are true, and not because they are the vogue. They do not wear thin with use nor are they outmoded with each new season. You can use them all the days of your life and not feel as though you'd been caught wearing that 1934 hat. Remember "So's your old man," with its simply killing alternative, "So's your Aunt Emma"? Remember "peachy" and "dandy" and "twenty-three, skidoo"? Well, then, you see what I mean. So—if sometimes we use "sympathetic" gut instead of "synthetic," when we put up our fly-rods in the spring, or "gore" ourselves on blueberries when they are "thick as spatter" along the road in August, or go to a beauty "saloon" to have our hair done just before Christmas, we may perhaps be excused on the grounds of human fallibility.

I like the subject matter of the conversation here, too. I like to sit around a fire and listen to slow, deep-toned talk of boats and guns and jumping a big buck one twilight over on the back side of Inlet Ridge, right where that jeesley swamp begins. I like descriptions of how the smelt ran in Mill Brook, spring before last—"You never see nawthin' like it. Looked like a big snake swimming up the current, they was so thick. Every dip, you'd net half a water-pail full"— and of the stately dance of a male spruce-partridge observed in a little sunny clearing, courting his demure brown hen— "She sat there like a bump on a log, never letting on she see him at all till he got disgusted and moseyed off into the bushes. She come to life then all right and skedaddled right along after him. Just like any woman." And all the male heads present nod in solemn agreement.

In one of these conclaves in front of an open fire in May, when snow was falling softly outside and all the animals were sleeping in, and there was a look and feel of November in the air, Albert Allen told us about the mice he once saw on the tent-site on the knoll just below Pondy Wangan. It has always seemed to me like a scene out of Hans Andersen, and why I don't really know. It's not much of a story. Perhaps it was the day. It had been spring, with the woods still and green and secret, full of the promise of freckled eggs and half-opened buds and unsheathing blossoms. Then in the middle of May we awoke to snow sifting gently down on the new elastic grass, and violets already in bloom, and on the white drift of the shagbush. It had been hot yesterday. To-day it was chill. We built a fire in the fireplace and let the dogs and the cats come in and resigned ourselves to a day indoors, an autumn day in May. It was a day that didn't count. You could think unreasonable thoughts and listen to and believe unlikely stories—and next day it would be spring again, and you'd be brisk and practical and efficient.

On the shank of the noon hour Albert Allen drifted in with his lunch under his arm. He wanted to dry his feet, and if it weren't too much bother to us, to bum a cup of coffee to drink with his cold sandwiches. Our lunch wasn't ready, but we sat around with him while he ate his, and that's when he told us about the mice. The chairs were all drawn up in a semicircle about the hearth, and the space in front was filled with long, sprawling wool-socked legs, and dozing dogs.

"I never saw anything like it," Albert said around his sandwich. "I came up over the knoll, walking quiet, and it looked as though the ground on that little square of grass were alive. There must have been two hundred deer mice there, milling around in circles. Don't know what they was going to do or was planning, because just about then I sneezed and the whole kit and caboodle of them vanished like a flash. There wasn't one to be seen in a second. But it sure was a queer, pretty sight while it lasted."

And it must have been. Deer mice are pretty anyhow, with their dainty ways, clean coloring, and big, inquisitive ears. To have run on a convention of them in the thin sunlight of spring must have been a strange and other-worldly experience—just the sort of experience to recount during an unseasonable May snowstorm. I told Albert so and offered him a bowl of pea soup, since our lunch was then ready. We have pea soup quite a lot, because we like it. I'm not a cook of any great distinction, but there are a few dishes with which I can cope, and pea soup is one of them.

This is my method. I take two cups of dried green split peas if I can get them, or yellow peas if I can't, and put them into a kettle with about three quarts of water. If I have a ham bone, I throw that in, too; but if I haven't, I take about eight slices of bacon, fry it crisp, break it into bits, and dump it and the fat, resultant of the frying, into the kettle. I add a large onion sliced thin, salt, pepper, and six whole cloves. Then I let the whole thing simmer for hours on the back of the stove. It has to be stirred rather often, because it has a tendency to catch. When the peas are cooked to a mush, I beat it vigorously with an egg beater to take out any roughness of texture, and serve it. Every woman must decide on the consistency she likes best. We like our soup rather thick, something that will line the ribs for a whole afternoon. But for thinner soup you can add more water at any point in the cooking, or for thicker soup you can cook it longer. It can be seen from the foregoing that I am not a scientific cook, given to exact measurements. This was a minor quarrel of Ralph's with me. He'd say, "This is good. Let's have it again."

And I'd say, "All right, if I can remember how I made it."

"But haven't you got your formula written down?" he'd ask, aghast.

And I'd have to say that no, I didn't have. I'd just thrown in anything that I thought suitable. I will admit that this method results in some sad failures; but it also results in some astounding successes which would never have been achieved under any other system.

Another thing that I do well is scrambled eggs. The first dish that Rufus ever specifically requested, at the age of three, was "eggs crashed in a pan and all messied up." That doesn't sound appetizing, but I guess it's as good a description of scrambled eggs as any. You really should have cream to do this dish right, but since I almost never do have, I use canned milk instead. You put the milk in a heavy iron or aluminum spider—or fry pan or skillet, depending on where you live—and break the eggs into it. About a scant half-cup of milk to an egg will do. Add salt and pepper and beat the eggs up with a fork, but not too much; just enough to break them up. The trick is never-never-never under any circumstances to allow the mixture to bubble. It has to be cooked slowly, on the back of the stove, and if you're in a hurry you'd better have some other kind of eggs. Every now and then you take a spoon and scrape with long, slow strokes the cooked layer of egg from the bottom of the pan, not breaking the yellow curls, but simply disengaging them. You continue this at intervals until the whole panful is cooked to a tender, moist consistency. Scrambled eggs can be awful—tough curds in a watery juice. But if you cook them with the care you'd give hummingbirds' tongues, they can be simply delicious.

I make the best fudge I ever ate, wrote she modestly. But I have witnesses who say it's the best fudge they ever ate, too. The recipe is standard: two cups of sugar, half a cup of rich milk, two squares of chocolate, salt, and butter the size of a walnut. Mix this up and place it in a saucepan on the back of the stove, in a fairly warm but definitely not hot spot. Then grease the pan into which you are eventually going to pour it, because if you don't do it then you will forget it until too late. You then—this sounds unhygienic, but it's the only test I know—dip your thumb and forefinger into the fudge mixture and rub them together. If you can't feel one single grain of the sugar unmelted, it's time to move the saucepan to the front of the stove and let it boil. Don't stir it any more than you have to—just enough to keep it from scorching. When it aprons off the spoon, it's time to start testing it in cold water. You know: drop a little into a dipper of water, and when it forms a soft ball, call it done. Take it off the stove, add a little vanilla, and start beating the living daylights out of it. The harder you beat, the better. When it thickens, watch and listen carefully. As soon as the surface takes on a dullish look and the sound of the beating spoon changes from a clop-clop to a slightly sucking note, it's time to pour it fast into the greased pan to cool. This is a very haphazard way to describe the steps, I know, but I don't know of any other way to convey what I mean. And in fairness I should add that I have for years tried to teach people to make fudge like mine, standing over them in a mother-hen manner through every inch of the process. Some have been good cooks and some have not, but they've all been willing and anxious. And not one has mastered the art. It's apparently just one of those things. But how did I ever get on the subject of cooking anyhow?

There are some other small things that I like about this life. I never saw snow fleas until I came here. I don't know that I'm particularly in love with them for themselves alone; but as sure as you see them, spring is just around the corner. The sight of them jumping about gives me a lift such as nothing else does. I feel, "There! We've weathered another winter. Pretty soon the snow will be shrinking and the ground will be bare in spots and it'll be time to paint the boats and go smelting and set up our fly-rods. We'll be having dandelion greens and digging in the garden. And the next thing we know, it'll be warm enough for swimming." I may be on snowshoes in the middle of a white world, looking down at a small patch of sunlit snow on a south bank, a patch lively with minute black specks; but it's spring already to me. I tell people about snow fleas, and half of them won't believe they exist until I show them. They are little fleas about half as large as dog fleas. They can hop prodigious distances in comparison to their size. I don't think that they bite and I don't think that they have any interest whatsoever in leaving the snow and inhabiting animals or people. What they eat or where they spend the winter or the summer I haven't the slightest idea. All I know about them is that one day when the sun is higher and warmer than it has been in long months they appear on the surface of the snow, hopping about at a great rate; and at the sight the heart swells and winter is over.

These are some of the things that make frozen water pails in the early morning, and kerosene lamps, and baths in galvanized wash tubs in front of the kitchen stove, and a climate of which it is said "We have two seasons: winter and Fourth of July" worth while for me. Thinking them over, I begin to wonder about my normality. They don't amount to so much, after all. Could it be possible that I am a very good example of arrested development?

CHAPTER XI

The Big Thing

A FEW MONTHS after Ralph died, a friend, who is older and wiser than I am, wrote me asking what I intended to do in the future, and I told him that I was going to try to go on with the life Ralph and I had planned for ourselves and our children, with the modifications made necessary by the fact that I was now alone. He was disapproving and a little disgusted, I think. "That's a chapter of your life that is over," he wrote back. "You've had some very valuable experiences and some very wonderful ones in that country, I know; but you are old enough and smart enough to realize that you can never recapture what once you had. It's time for you to move on, to live a fuller life. You don't have to stay stuck in the woods. Keep the place to come back to for a short time summers if you want to, but go somewhere else. Spend your winters in Arizona, for example, or go to the West Indies. Spend a month each year in New York, where you'll find mental stimulation. Don't bury yourself in that place through a mistaken sense of loyalty. Use your good sense and get out."

At first I was angry, but then I realized that he was speaking in behalf of what he honestly considered my best interests. The trouble was that he didn't understand.

252

He didn't understand that this is not a place where I live from necessity or for want of a better. This is my country, my home. This is the place into which I have put too much of time and hard work and thought and love ever to leave voluntarily. What would I be doing in Arizona or Venezuela —or the Garden of the Hesperides, for that matter? I'd be thinking that about now the ice must be getting ready to go out, and the smelts should be running; or that now is the time of the first snowfall and the best deer hunting; or that travel on the lake must be getting pretty tough by now. I'd be wondering who was logging on Elephant Back this winter, and whether Larry had got his ice in yet, and what work was being done on the dams. I'd be reading the home town paper and listening to weather reports on the radio, trying to find out whether there were blizzards blanketing Maine to-day, or this was the week of the January Thaw. I'd be wishing I were home.

But it's more than homesickness. There is a poem by Roy Helton that says what I mean. It's called "Lonesome Water," and goes in part:

> Drank lonesome water:
> Warn't but a tad then
> Up in the laurel thick
> Digging for sang;
> Came on a place where
> The stones were hollow;
> Something below them
> Tinkled and rang.
>
> Dug where I heard it
> Drippling below me;
> Should a knowd better,
> Should a been wise;

Leant down and drank it
Clutching and gripping
The over hung cliv
With the ferns in my eyes.

I'd drunk lonesome water
I knowed in a minute:
Never larnt nothing
From then till to-day:
Nothing worth larning
Nothing worth knowing.
I'm bound to the hills
And I can't get away.*

That's how it is with me. It's more than loving the land.
It's more than enjoying the life. It is after all not an easy
land to love and many people find it terrifying. Maeterlinck
has suggested the profound antagonism that nature feels for
her renegade step-child, man, and this is an antagonism
which cannot be ignored in the woods as it can on city streets
peopled with men. Man is important among his own crea-
tions; he is lord of the earth. In this country you cannot
avoid the knowledge that man is a pretty small potato in
the natural scheme. If every man on earth were to die, the
ants would still excavate and inhabit their elaborate sub-
terranean palaces and continue their communistic way of
life. Snakes would sun themselves on the frost-heaved rocks
of man's now meaningless walls. Wasps would go on manu-
facturing paper and building nests under the eaves—the
short while eaves still remained—with never a moment's inconvenience. Horses and cattle, free of bondage, would roam
over the land. The insensate things—the grass and the weeds

* From *Lonesome Water* by Roy Helton. Copyright, 1930, by Harper &
Brothers.

and the trees—would soon cover up all trace of man's tenancy of the earth, creeping silently and inexorably forward, inch by inch, until the last road was overgrown and the last cultivated patch of ground erased.

Of these things you are intellectually aware, living in a city, if you ever stop to think of them; but there is no need to think of them there. In this country you know them to the marrow of your bones, you are constantly reminded of them, because you have to fight daily and desperately against ants ruining the garden, and porcupines gnawing at the underpinning of the house, and deer-mice stealing the last of the corn meal. You have to spend weeks of each year cutting back the brush from the carry, and weeding the strawberry bed, and repelling the forest's invasion on the clearing. You know that nature hates you and is intent upon your annihilation. To some this is a burden of intolerable weight upon the spirit. And to some the pleasures of this life do not compensate for the drudgery, the inconvenience, the discomfort, the going-without and making-do that it involves. Possibly nobody in his right mind would choose to live under conditions of open warfare and almost constant physical hardship; but those who have drunk lonesome water are not in their right minds. They have no choice. They are under a compulsion for which there is no therapy.

But it's even more than that. It seems to me that the thing for which you spend your life to build, if you would be whole, is not a bank account, or an unimpeachable social position, or success in any one of a thousand lines of endeavor; it seems to me that the only thing worth having is a certainty of yourself, a complete confidence in how you will act under any circumstances, a *knowledge* of yourself. People who have this knowledge are people who have kept their edges intact, people with what I can only call *core;* by which I guess I mean the indestructible skeleton of character, showing through manner and mannerism, as good bones show through flesh. It's the thing you know you can count on in yourself and in others, and it's not easily acquired. Here in this country I have found the circumstances and conditions that will make a woman of me if anything ever will. Here I have my feet on the solid earth, literally, and that is good; for it seems to me that the earth is the only permanence we can know. In spite of war and pestilence and destruction, in spite of the unthinkable cruelties man inflicts upon man, in spite of political upheavals and personal disloyalties and treacheries, the earth remains unchanged. The grass grows and the rivers run downhill and the wild berry bushes bear fruit, each in its season. The earth can be depended upon, and unless you take your stance upon a certainty, how can the structure of your life be anything but precarious, a house built upon sand?

My friends say of me, "Poor foolish Louise! Think of her living way up there in that God-forsaken place. Why, she never even goes to the movies and she hasn't a decent rag to her name. She's still wearing that tweed suit she bought five years ago, whenever she has to appear in public. It was a good enough suit in its day, but— She slops around all the time in slacks and shirts. And she works so hard. Heavens, she looks five years older than she is, and there's no need of it. She doesn't have to deprive herself like that."

Oh, but there is need of it! I have to live here, if I can ever hope to be the sort of person I would like to be. And I have learned that there is no such thing as sacrifice for me, when it comes to living in this country, because there is nothing in the world that I can deprive myself of—clothes, food, entertainment, anything you can mention—that means anything at all compared to the deprivation of leaving the land and the life that I love and of which I am a part. It would be the wrong land and the wrong life for many who are seeking the same things that I am seeking. Every individual must find the proper ground on which to work out his own salvation. For some it is city; for some it is farm; for some it is laboratory or monastery or tropical jungle. The important thing is to find the place in which you can be the best person you are capable of being, in which you can develop your potentialities most nearly to the utmost; and the implication is that that is the place in which you can be most useful and happiest, the place in which you feel at home. I have found my place.

And still I haven't said what I meant to say, and I guess I never will say it. It doesn't make much difference anyhow. Every book is as many books as it has readers, plus one. The author—who is the one—writes about what he sees or feels as truthfully as he can, words being the faulty conveyors of thought that they are; but his book is a different book to everyone who reads it, since every man interprets the written word in the light of his own experience and nature. No two men are alike, nor are their backgrounds. Therefore no book hews to a line, but is a fluid thing, all things to all men. Were I to be blessed with the tongue of men and of angels, which is highly improbable, still no one in all the world would read what I had written in the light in which I wrote it. This in the long run is my gain, for men and women of greater understanding than I possess read into what I have written meanings that I am incapable of conceiving. Undoubtedly I'd be smart just to let it ride and get on with the business in hand.

One of the many good things about growing older is that things are not what they seem. The loaf of bread you baked this morning is not just another loaf of bread, to be eaten with appropriate comment for dinner. It's composed in part of the first bread you ever tried to make, which for some obscure reason wouldn't rise a sixty-fourth of an inch. After two days of babying it, you slapped it into a moderate oven in the pious hope that maybe it would turn out all right after all. It baked through and through and through, slowly attaining the appearance and tender succulence of well-fired brick. You offered it to the family, and they loyally tried to hack off a slice. No go. So you gave it to the dogs. Hungry as they were—and young huskies are always hungry—and sharp though their fangs, they finally gave it up as a bad job, after no more than marring the surfaces. So you threw it out on the dump, thinking that after a month of weathering it would be soft enough to tempt some starving porcupine or bear. In the spring when the snow had wasted away, you surprised a big gaunt buck eating cardboard boxes that had been thrown out during the winter, while the bread lay around his feet, intact. It lies there to this day, for all you know. To-day's loaf of bread is the bread you made once with the last flour in the house, when you had no money to buy more—the bread the dogs stole and ate in dough form when your back was turned for a minute. You shed tears over that bread. It's the salt-risin' bread you attempted once when you ran out of yeast. It was salt all right, but risin'? Unh-*unh!* It's the marvelous batch of bread that you finally achieved in an offhand moment when you were thinking about something else. All the bread you ever made and all the people who ever ate it are implicit in the sponge under your hands as you knead and toss and pound.

And so it is with everything. Every experience contains not only the present but the past as well, amplifying, and enriching it. I do not believe in living in the past alone. Life has a present and a future as well. But neither do I believe that it is possible or desirable to try to cut the past away from the present. Whatever you are, whatever life you lead, is a result of the experiences of the past, and to attempt to divorce the Now from the Then is foolish and I would say dangerous. Institutions are full of people who have been incapable of assimilating their pasts and building their lives out of the materials therein provided.

No, I can't recapture what once I had. My friend was right. But I don't want to recapture it. The past recaptured isn't growth. It's the preserving under glass domes of things which should have been allowed to ripen into productive maturity. The past means nothing unless its promise is fulfilled in the future.